WHISKY

—THE MANUAL—

WHISKY

— THE MANUAL —

— DAVE BROOM —

MITCHELL BEAZLEY

An Hachette UK Company
www.hachette.co.uk

First published in Great Britain in 2014
by Mitchell Beazley, an imprint of
Octopus Publishing Group Limited, Carmelite
House, 50 Victoria Embankment, London EC4Y 0DZ
www.octopusbooks.co.uk

Distributed in the US by Hachette Book Group
1290 Avenue of the Americas, 4th and 5th Floors,
New York, NY 10020
Distributed in Canada by Canadian Manda Group
664 Annette Street, Toronto, Ontario,
Canada M6S 2C8

Specially commissioned photography by
Cristian Barnett.

ISBN: 978 1 84533 755 1

A CIP record for this book is available from the
British Library.

Set in Champion, Foundry Sterling, Gotham and
Old Press Regular.

Printed and bound in China.

10 9 8 7 6 5 4

Note The spelling "whisky" is used for all whisky
styles throughout this book except for American
and Irish, for which the spelling "whiskey" is used.

Head of Editorial Tracey Smith
Senior Editor Leanne Bryan
Copy Editor Hilary Lumsden
Proofreader Jamie Ambrose
Indexer Cathy Heath
Art Director Jonathan Christie
Executive Art Editor Juliette Norsworthy
Designer Geoff Fennell
Bartender Ryan Chetiyawardana
Picture Research Manager Giulia Hetherington
Production Controller Sarah Kramer
Bottle Shot Research Ella McLean

CONTENTS

INTRODUCTION

This is a book about how to drink whisky. To be (slightly) more precise, this is a book about how whisky has been enjoyed down the centuries, and it offers ideas on how to maximize pleasure when you next look at an off-licence shelf or back bar. That's simple, you might think – open the bottle, take a glass and pour liquid into it... and remember to open your mouth when bending your elbow. Well, yes – and no.

EXPLODING MYTHS

People have always drunk whisky neat, but at any time when it reached its greatest heights of popularity it was a drink that was consumed mixed or drunk long – as a Toddy, in a Julep or a Sling, as a Punch, a cocktail or a Highball. As I write, whisky of every stripe is enjoying unparalleled success around the world – and guess what? The way that most of the new converts to its charms prefer to take it is mixed. It is only in the mature markets where the (actually rather recent) notion that it must be taken neat – and with a grimace – clings tenaciously on.

It is just one of a few myths that have sprung up around whisky, revolving around how to drink it, when to drink it, at what age you can start to appreciate it, and what sex you have to be. These need to be swept away, because when you examine them they are all negative. None encourage people to drink whisky, they only give reasons why NOT to drink it. Now, I'm no marketing expert, but that doesn't strike me as a particularly clever way to try to sell yourself.

Around the world, people are finding new ways to enjoy whisky.

Hang on, you might say, I thought you said whisky was booming? It is, but it is doing so in countries where these myths are being ignored. Plus, when you compare whisky's volume to vodka, you can see that there is plenty of scope for new drinkers to be converted.

Whisky isn't for an elite, it is for everyone. It's a great drink, a fascinating drink, a complex drink, a historical drink but it is, ultimately, JUST A DRINK. Whisky's inability to dispatch the myths associated with it is one reason why it can remain a difficult sell. So it's time to take aim and blast them away.

Myth 1: Whisky is old-fashioned

You can picture the scene. There they sit in their armchairs, a group of men, tweed-suited, perhaps be-kilted and picking at their sporrans, a glass of golden spirit in a crystal tumbler at their side. Occasionally they'll mutter to each other about peat and glower at the noisy young folk behind them, drinking their fancy mixed drinks. That's most folks' image of whisky. Backs to the world, human wagons drawn into a leather-armchaired circle repelling the barbarians. Old-fashioned. Irrelevant. The same applies to bourbon, just with less tweed and kilts.

In 1970s Britain, America, and Japan, Scotch and bourbon both faltered, resulting in two generations for whom whisky has been an unknown entity. Because of low levels of investment, whisky was never made contemporary and relevant.

To see how false this old-fashioned image is, you need only look at what is happening in bars and restaurants elsewhere in the world – there's precious little old-school about the way whisky is being consumed in São Paulo or Mexico City. Say it's a grandfather's drink to the hipsters in Taipei, Shanghai or Moscow and you'll be looked at as if you are crazy. It's not whisky that is old-fashioned, it's our attitude toward it.

Myth 2: Whisky is a drink for old men

Let's go back to our (mythic) bar. A woman walks in and orders a whisky. The old chaps fall out of their armchairs in astonishment.

If you try telling master blender Kirsteen Campbell that women can't enjoy whisky, you'd better make sure you have your running shoes on.

"Woman! Know your place," one splutters.

"Don't be harsh," says another. "Now, my dear," he says, "This is a strong drink. Maybe start with something nice and light, eh?" He pats her on the head and winks at the barman. "Get her a white wine instead. I'll pay. "

The days when it was believed that whisky was too strong to be appreciated by "pretty little things with fluff between their ears" have gone. So, hopefully, have the embarrassing attempts to market whisky at women, which usually ended up with either pink whisky, or something sweet and light "for the ladies". This, as well as being wildly patronizing, still infers that women can't quite cope with full-blooded whisky flavours, which is far from true.

Look around the world. In every new market as many women are drinking whisky as men. Try telling master blenders like Maureen Robinson and Caroline Martin (Diageo), Rachel Barrie (Morrison Bowmore), Stephanie MacLeod (Dewar's) and Kirsteen Campbell (Cutty Sark) that whisky is a man's drink. You'd better have some good running shoes on.

Whisky has the widest range of styles and flavours of any wood-aged spirit. It is versatile. It is for everyone.

Myth 3: Whisky should be drunk neat
Here's a true story. I'm in a taxi in Glasgow and strike up a conversation with the driver, who discovers that I write about whisky. He then regales me about his recent trip to a distillery. "I've never been much of a whisky drinker – I hate that burn – but you know what? At the end of the tour they said I was allowed to add a wee drop of water to the dram. It was beautiful!"

So here's a 50-something-year-old Scottish guy who has been told for, say, 36 years (this is Glasgow) that it's wrong to add water to whisky and, as a result, hated the drink. How many people have been told the same over the years, tried neat whisky and never repeated the exercise? Probably millions.

This is hardly a one-off. At a dinner with top chaps from the advertising industry I suggested that they'd like to add water to the whisky in front of them. There was a sense of mild consternation at this notion. "Are you allowed to do that?" asked one. "Of course!"

I replied. They did, they smiled and had another... and another. "You know," said one to me later, "after all these years of drinking whisky I've never before been given permission to add water."

Permission? Here were highly respected, highly intelligent men who had been drinking whisky for years but had never enjoyed it because no one had told them that water is a friend, not the enemy.

Adding water not only releases aromas, but allows flavours to spread gently over the tongue and kills the burn. If the aim is to get more people to try whisky, then why are we still stuck in this mentality that pain is better than pleasure? Drink your whisky long with water or soda, throw ginger ale at it, try it with green tea or coconut water, make a cocktail. Use its flavours to make compelling drinks that make you smile.

Myth 4: Whisky is for after dinner
We're back in our bar, which is "fireflied with whisky glasses" as poet Norman MacCaig memorably put it. The meal has been taken and it is time to relax with a glass. It's a throwback to another Victorian habit of gentlemen retiring for whisky and cigars and women doing whatever Victorian women did – take laudanum, perhaps. Neither happens these days.

The combination of drink-driving regulations and restaurants' aversion to offering digestifs has brought down the curtain on this ideal whisky-drinking ritual, which is a real shame, as the slow sipping of a post-prandial ardent spirit is good both for the digestion and for conversation. Because whisky, in recent years, was seen only as a post-dinner drink, when that occasion disappeared, so did another reason to drink the spirit.

In this case it's worth taking a tip from the Victorians. Ladies and gentlemen... I give you the Highball as an ideal pre-dinner drink. I challenge you to say that a cold Highball made with peaty whisky and charged water isn't as refreshing as a bucket of Pinot Grigio. If you want other options, there are 500 later on in the book.

Myth 5: Single malts are better than blends
One of the prime reasons for the decline in popularity of the whisky apéritif has been the fall (in mature

markets) in blends and the emergence of the paradigm: malts are good, blends are bad. Blends are seen as inferior/representing a dilution of character/rough/cheap/"inauthentic".

Yet whisky's growth in new markets isn't being led by malts. For Brazilians, Mexicans, Russians, South Africans, Chinese, and Vietnamese, "whisky" = blends.

We have to stop thinking of blends and malts as being the same. All of these great single-malt distilleries wouldn't exist were it not for blends. Scotland wouldn't be a global producer if it were solely reliant on the inevitably limited production of 105 individual single-malt distilleries.

Blends are different to malts. They have always been driven by occasion – who is drinking it, when they're drinking it, and how they're drinking it. They are also driven by flavour. In 1850, just prior to the emergence of blends, Scotch was struggling because the flavours of single malts were too idiosyncratic. Blending these individuals together retained complexity, but gave a final flavour with wider appeal. Did someone say mass-market? I know! Imagine being genuinely popular. Terrible, isn't it?

Myth 6: Scotland makes the best whisky

Scotch remains the largest whisky category, but to say Scotland automatically makes the best whisky would be categorically wrong. Scotland makes the best Scotch. So don't dismiss the resurgent Irish whiskey category with its characteristic juicy, succulent, and glorious drinkability; or Japan whose precise, complex single malts are seen as the new kids on the block – despite the fact that the industry in Japan is 90 years old; or the hugely exciting world of bourbon, rye, and Canadian whiskies.

Then stir in whiskies from Wales, England, Australia, India, Taiwan, France, Sweden, and the growing craft-distilling movement in America. Think of that for a second. If this spirit is dead in the water, then why are so many people internationally building distilleries to make a drink that, one might assume, no one would ever consume? Time to re-evaluate. Whisky is back. The only rule now is: Enjoy!

Japan's whiskies are winning many international awards.

HISTORY

This book is about how to enjoy whisky. This history, therefore, concentrates on how whisky has been consumed over the centuries and how the spirit has worked its way into the lives, hearts, and words of the cultures where it has been made and drunk.

SCOTLAND & IRELAND 1200–1745

So, who was it? The person who had the inspired notion to take beer and boil it in a still? For Scottish author Neil M Gunn, it was a Celtic shaman. For some it was a man of the cloth; for others, one from a list of alchemists. Let's start with them. Charlatans, conjurers, and snake-oil salesman, or proto-chemists, questers, mystics, seekers after truth? How did their investigations into distillation, which started in Persia with the works of Jabir (721–815), al-Kindi (801–873) and Rhazes (865–925), end up on the Celtic fringes?

Initially it was through the work of Robert of Chester in Segovia in 1144, who translated their texts into Latin, and also thanks to Michael Scot (born in the Scottish Borders around 1175, died in Italy around 1236) who studied and learned Arabic in Toledo and became the court astrologer to Frederick II in Salerno. Scot translated works such as Rhazes' major alchemical work, *Liber Luminis Luminum*, and was therefore cogniscent of distillation.

Although a passing mention in Dante's *Inferno* is all that remains of the life's work of the first Scottish distiller, it's widely agreed that distilling beer is a Celtic invention. Not so. The first reference to beer being distilled in Britain comes in Chaucer's *The Canterbury Tales* (1378–1400). In "The Canon's Yeoman's Tale", the narrator reveals the secrets of alchemy, his master's "slippery... elvish art". The talk is of alembics and heat, of a complex list of ingredients and process, including "oille of tartre, alum glas, berme, wort..." Beer distilled.

It is perhaps surprising that another century passed before there was any reference to grain being distilled in Scotland. Enter Brother John Cor, the most widely known – yet invisible – Scotsman in history. His name is mentioned once, in 1494's exchequer rolls of King James IV of Scotland, when Brother Cor receives his "eight bolls of malt to make aqua vitae" (water of life).

The art of distillation started with alchemical investigations.

BOECE'S GARDEN AQUA VITAE

I decided to make a modern homage to Boece's ancestral beverage. Although he didn't specify what went into this, some research into medieval Scottish gardens gave a list of likely ingredients. Bartender Ryan Chetiyawardana and I then tried to rotovap (vacuum-distil) a selection of these. The result was not exactly a triumph. Undaunted, we then steeped the herbal base: marjoram, basil, lavender, sage, and rosemary, in new-make spirit and cooked it *sous-vide* (I know, both of these techniques were beyond Boece, but needs must). The result was a fragrant, bright-green drink with appropriately herbal notes. A small adjustment with heather honey was all that was needed.

Who he was we know not, where he was domiciled is a mystery, but at least we know that he was making aqua vitae from malted grain, perhaps to help his king in a continuation of the works of Scot.

It is hardly credible that the distilling of beer took a century to reach the grain-rich lands north of the border, more unlikely still when you consider the importance of the MacBeathads (anglicized as Beatons), who arrived on Islay in 1300 with the Ulster princess Aine o'Cathain. Known as *ollamhs*, they were masters of medicine, court physicians to every Scottish king from Robert the Bruce (1306) to Charles I (1625). A Beaton was physician to James IV.

As "staunch Arabians" the Beatons followed the herbal-based, alchemical medical principles of Avicenna and Averroës (initially translated in part into Latin by Michael Scot, and then into Gaelic in the 14th century by the Beatons themselves). Distillation for the Beatons was medicinal. They are the root. Brother Cor? An extra.

Writing in *The History and Chronicles of Scotland* in 1527, Hector Boece, the first principal of Aberdeen University, offers a different perspective on whisky:

"When my ancestors were determined of a set purpose to be merie, they used a kind of aqua vite [sic], void of all spice, and onelie consisting of such herbs and roots as grew in their own gardens…"

The "authorized version" of whisky history states that whisky was first a medicine and that it took centuries to change into a potable drink. But Boece shows the opposite. This is a spirit that has been made to be enjoyed, and in a fashion that has been handed down. His ancestors drank it for pleasure, conceivably at the same time as Brother Cor was labouring over his eight bolls.

It is unlikely that Boece and his ancestors would distil expensive imported wine when there was ale at hand – and they were clearly trying to keep the costs down by not using imported spices. Rather they opened their windows and let the scents of the garden inspire them.

These herbs would have been a mix of the cultivated (hyssop, marjoram, lavender) and local (wild mountain thyme, rosemary, rowan berry, and heather, the last maybe in the form of honey from the hills). Boece's aqua vitae is a spirit of place, scented with the bloom of the land. It is rooted in the Scottish landscape, the ingredients selected as a conscious choice because of their flavour.

It was the Irish, however, who were to become famed for this type of whisky. Gentleman traveller Fynes Moryson wrote:

> "Usquebaugh... [is] preferred before our own [English] aqua vitae because of the mingling of Raysons, Fennell seede and other things, mitigating the heat and makeing the taste pleasant..."

Moryson knew of what he was writing. He was the first of a group of writers who would provide wayposts on whisky's journey. His four-volume *Itinerary*, which was published in 1617, is the account of a decade of wanderings in Europe, which included his discovery in Ireland of this new spirit.

The recipe is fascinating – the imported and local used together – as is the name. The "authorized version" tells us that aqua vitae, when translated into Gaelic, became usquebaugh (actually *uisge beatha*), which then became corrupted into usky/whisky. In fact, usquebaugh and whisky are two different drinks. The former is flavoured, the latter is clear and hot, coming straight off the still.

Moryson was travelling at the time of the Nine Years War, which saw King James I take control of Ulster and place his cronies into positions of power. Among them was Sir Thomas Phillips, who, in 1608, was given the sole right to distil in "o'Cahane's county" – named after the ancestors of Aine o'Cathain.

What is overlooked is what Sir Thomas was permitted to make, namely: "*acquavitae* [sic]*, usquabagh* [sic] and *aqua composita*". In other words, he was allowed to distil neat whisky, whisky that had been redistilled with flavourings, and whisky that had had flavourings macerated in it. Three different styles, not one.

For close on 300 years, usquebaugh was to become an admired, complex drink that appeared in the distillation books for the landed gentry, such as the example from the early 17th century (*see* box, p.16). It is notable because of the addition of the ingredient that came to define the drink – saffron.

Clearly anything involving saffron isn't a drink of the peasant class, but Meg Dods' "Usquebaugh, The Irish

TWO USQUEBAUGHS

ROYAL USQUEBAUGH
(The Complete Distiller,
A Cooper, 1757)

"Take of Cinnamon, Ginger and Coriander-seed, of each three Ounces; Nutmegs four Ounces and a Half; Mace, Cloves and Cubebs each once Ounce and a Half. Bruise these Ingredients and put them into an Alembic with eleven Gallons of Proof spirit, and two Gallons of Water; and distil till the Faints begin to rise; fastening four ounces and a half of English Saffron tied in a cloth to the end of the worm. Take Raisins stoned four Pounds, and a Half; Dates three Pounds, Liquorice root sliced two Pounds; digest these twelve hours in two gallons of water; strain out the clear Liquor, add it to that obtained by Distillation, and dulcify the whole with fine Sugar. (This makes 10 gallons.)"

USQUEBAUGH, THE IRISH CORDIAL
(The Cook and Housewife's Manual,
Meg Dods, 1829)

"To two quarts of whisky without a smoky taste put a pound of stoned raisins, a half-ounce of nutmegs, a quarter-ounce of cloves, the same quantity of cardamoms, all bruised in a mortar; the rind of a Seville orange, rubbed off on lumps of sugar, a little tincture of saffron, and half a pound of brown candy-sugar. Shake the infusion every day for a fortnight and filter for use. *Obs* Not a drop of water should be put into Irish Cordial. It is sometimes tinged a fine green with the juice of spinage, instead of the saffron tint, from which it takes the name (as we conjecture) of usquebeae or *yellow water*."

Cordial" (*see* box, left) contains a teasing suggestion about how that colouring issue could be surmounted by tinging the spirit "a fine green with the juice of spinage".

There's no evidence of flavouring in 1703, when another gentleman traveller, Martin Martin, writes of his journeys in the western islands of Scotland. Other names appear in his description of the whiskies of Lewis however: usquebaugh, triple-distilled trestarig and four-times distilled usquebaugh-baul. Clearly, while other parts of Scotland had followed in Boece's and their Irish cousins' footsteps, the locals had their own take. What he did find out, however, was how whisky was being consumed:

> "It is called in their language a *Streah*, i.e. a round, for the company sat in a circle, the cup-bearer filled the drink round to them, and all was drunk out whatever the liquor was, whether strong or weak; they continued drinking sometimes twenty-four sometimes forty-eight hours..."

You can look at this in two ways: as a drunken debauch, or as a way for a community to gather democratically – in a circle – and bind themselves together through the passing and sharing of the common cup. At this moment we see that whisky has ceased to be just alcohol and has become part of a nation's culture. Long rooted in the flavours of the hills, it is now rooted in community. That is not to say it's not being consumed enthusiastically.

> "Some of the Highland gentlemen are immoderate drinkers of usky; even three or four quarts at a sitting..."

Such was the scene that met Captain Edmund Burt when he toured Scotland in 1726, clutching his lemons so that he could make Punch, and as a gift to his hosts. As well as finding that whisky was drunk out of, possibly decorated, scallop shells, he must have been relieved to find that while the early 18th-century Highland version of Punch avoided citrus, it existed as a drink:

> "[they] mixed it with water and honey, or with milk and honey; at other times the mixture is only the aqua vitae, sugar and butter; this they burn till the butter and sugar are dissolved."

The volumes of drink mentioned by Captain Burt also suggests that dilution was commonplace.

By the 18th century, whisky-drinking was a convivial, social experience.

Whisky was becoming part of daily life. As Doctor Johnson was to note later in the century:

"A man of the Hebrides... as soon as he appears in the morning, swallows a glass of whisky; ... they are not a drunken race... but no man is so abstemious as to refuse the morning dram, which they call a skalk [which comes from Gaelic *sgailc*, a blow to the head]."

Consumption has become ritualized: it is sacrament, payment, the cornerstone of hospitality. Whisky is taken on waking in the darkness before dawn and before sleep at night. It is in the smoothed wood or horn of the quaich being passed around at celebrations, the scallop shell, the sweetened burn, drinking in the round.

SCOTLAND & IRELAND 1745–1850

Yet the days of the rural ritual were under threat. From the mid-18th century, whisky-making in Scotland and Ireland began to shift from small-scale production to commercial distillation. With it came a blizzard of legislation, as the government tried to control excessive consumption while maximizing revenue – and failed.

By the end of the 18th century, distillers in the Scottish Lowlands, many of them members of the linked Haig and Stein dynasty, were prospering. Their eyes were on the potential riches available from exporting their lower-cost spirit to London to be rectified into gin.

By 1786, however, legislation had forced the Lowland distillers to slash prices to below cost simply to survive. Inevitably, many didn't. In addition, they were now being taxed on the capacity of their stills, a move that they tried to sidestep by designing saucer-like pots with shallow bodies and tall, skinny necks that could be "discharged at a rate of once every two minutes and three quarters". Initially, the rank nature of the subsequent spirit didn't matter when it was rectified into gin, but when the export trade collapsed, the only option was to flood the Lowland shebeens with it.

As Robert Burns wrote in a letter from 1788, "The whisky of this country [Lowlands] is a most rascally liquor; and by consequence only drunk by the most rascally part of the inhabitants." Burns was right in considering the Lowlands and Highlands (and islands) as different countries. In 1784, the excise drew a line that separated Scotland into two parts, each with its own legislation. North of the Highland Line, the government

By the early 19th century, large-scale commercial distilleries were being built in Scotland and Ireland.

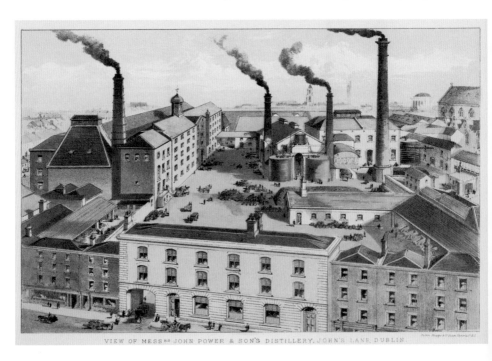

VIEW OF MESS^{RS} JOHN POWER & SON'S DISTILLERY, JOHN'S LANE, DUBLIN.

was trying, clumsily, to impose commercial distilling on a system that was the preserve of farmers using their own crops to make their own whisky in small stills. The new legislation effectively made this impossible.

In addition, though the Highland whisky was of better quality than that coming from the Steins' saucers, and though demand for it rose, legal export to the south was banned. There was only one solution. Whisky-making went underground, with landlords ignoring their tenants' activities in order to keep them on the land. The moonshiners were concentrated in Glen Livet, Kintyre, and Islay – all of them remote and hard to patrol, but with good transport links to the Lowland markets.

A similar situation existed in Ireland. By 1779, there were 1,228 registered distilleries but, the same year when the law taxing stills on their capacity was brought in, 982 simply disappeared! The remaining "Parliamentary distilleries", like their colleagues in the Scottish Lowlands, made an unpalatable liquor, driving up demand for the illicit potion.

In 1823, after an agreement that landowners would uphold the law if more equable legislation was introduced, the situation in both countries changed. The Highland Line was scrapped, duty was halved, there was a rebate for using 100 per cent malt, stills had to be at least 40 gallons, and duty-free warehousing was permitted, as were exports.

This wasn't the start of legal whisky distilling in Scotland. What the change in law did was usher capital into distilling. Whisky had become a business. Its serves, however, were still more adventurous than often believed. Elizabeth Grant of Rothiemurchus wrote of her life as a "Highland Lady" in the 1820s:

> "Decent gentlewomen begin the day with a dram... In our house, the bottle of whisky, with the accompaniment of a silver salver of small glasses, was placed on the side table with cold meats every morning."

Whisky may have become the drink of the urban poor, but Highland whisky was acquiring a certain upper-class respectability. Nothing brings this home more than George IV's demands on his visits to Ireland (1821) and Scotland the year after. He said in Dublin:

"I assure you, dear friends, I have an Irish heart and
will this night give a proof of my affection towards
you... by drinking your health with a bumper of
whisky punch."
(Note, not neat whisky.)

When the King then visited Edinburgh and again asked
for whisky, the call went out for a bottle of (then illicit)
Glenlivet. This was supplied with considerable reluctance
by the ever-peevish Elizabeth Grant. She records:

"My father sent word to me... to empty my pet
bin, where there was whisky long in wood, long
in uncorked bottles, mild as milk, and the true
contraband *goût* in it."

The King's conversion to whisky has more than a touch
of spin to it. Whatever George's true motivation, this era
saw the Whisky Toddy becoming a drink for gentlemen.
In 1864 Charles Tovey wrote in *British and Foreign Spirits*:

"You will find Toddy at the after-dinner tables of the
aristocracy, mingling its fumes with the odours of
Lafitte [sic] or Romanee Conti...; it is customary, after
dinner, to bring in the Whisky, hot water and sugar,
which each person brews according to his taste..."

Whisky Punch, also served warm – this is Scotland!
– was still drunk, and a cunning local solution had been
found to the lack of lemons. Writing in 1772, another
gentleman traveller, Thomas Pennant, revealed that
rowan berries were used to enhance its flavour:

"The people of the Hebrides extract an acid for
punch from the berries of the mountain ash."

WHISKY PUNCH

**THE ETTRICK SHEPHERD'S
HOT WHISKY-PUNCH**
(*Noctes Ambrosiane
Part Three*, 1828–30)

Noctes Ambrosiane is a
collection of encounters
written at the start of the 19th
century by Professor John
Wilson, with help from other
Edinburgh luminaries, such as
the poet James Hogg (aka "The
Ettrick Shepherd"), in which
they, in fictionalized form,
discuss the ways of the world
and the strangeness of life.

The directions for making
"Whisky-Punch" come in a
footnote to the piece in which
Hogg is actually making
a Whisky Toddy. "...it's an
instinck wi' m noo," he says,
"making het whisky toddy. A'
the time o our silly discourse...
I was steerin' about the liquid,
plumpin in the bits o sugar and
garrin' the green bottle gurgle."
The footnote expands on this:
"The mystery of making
whisky-punch comes with
practice. The sugar should
first be dissolved with a small

quantity of water, which
must be what the Irish call
"screeching hot". Next throw
in the whisky. Then add a thin
shaving of lemon peel. Then
add the rest of the water, so
that the spirits shall be a third
of the mixture. Lastly, drink!
Lemon juice is deleterious and
should be eschewed."
For the reasons behind the
apparent Caledonian aversion
to citrus juice, turn to the
Cocktails chapter (*see* pages
184–219).

HIGHLAND BITTERS

BITTERS: AN EXCELLENT TONIC
(*The Cook and Housewife's Manual*,
Meg Dods, 1829)

"Take of juniper berries two
ounces, of gentian root one
ounce and a half or coriander
seeds a quarter of an ounce, of
calamus-aromaticus a quarter of
an ounce, of snake-root a drachm,
and of cardamom seeds a half-
drachm. Cut the gentian root into
small pieces, pound the other
ingredients in a mortar and put
the whole into a large bottle or
jar with five bottles of the best
malt-whisky of the strength of
glass proof (or 15 per cent below
hydrometer proof). Shake the
bottle a little when the ingredients
are first put in but not afterwards.
Let it stand for twelve days
carefully corked and then strain it
off and bottle it for use." A slightly
adapted (less insanely bitter)
version of this recipe is found in the
Cocktails chapter (*see* page 187).

The final member of Scotland's whisky triumvirate was bitters. This was first defined in 1808 in Jamieson's *Dictionary of the Scottish Language* as "a dram much used in the Highlands as a stomachic, made from an infusion of aromatic herbs and whisky" and was something that, according to Sir Archibald Geikie a century later, was "often to be found on Highland sideboards in the morning".

That whisky wasn't solely a neat spirit is underlined by a number of recipes in Meg Dods' *The Cook and Housewife's Manual*, which includes (almond-based) Scotch Noyau, Cherry whisky, Usquebaugh, Norfolk Punch, Bitters, and Scotch Het-Pint (in which whisky, hot ale, sugar, and beaten eggs are "briskly poured from one vessel to another till it becomes smooth and bright" before being carried in a hot copper kettle).

Why did whisky acquire this growing respectability in its native land? That "contraband *goût*" had a powerful allure. As Tovey says:

"Until the distillation of whisky was prohibited in the Highlands it was never drunk at gentleman's tables."

Whisky had also acquired a wider cultural resonance. Macpherson's publication of the ancient Ossian poetic saga in 1760 saw a re-imagining of Scotland through a stitching together and sentimentalizing of myth. Ossian's success shows the void at the heart of Scottish psyche and the need to rediscover a lost past – or a palimpsest of it. Whisky was a liquid metaphor for this romantic view of Scotland. Drink it and you bought into the myth.

The debate as to what it meant to be Scottish was central to the writings of Fergusson, Burns, Hogg, and Scott and underpins the Scottish Renaissance, during which Edinburgh-based intellectuals were redrawing the world in geology (Hutton), philosophy (Hume), and economics (Adam Smith), asking what it is to be human and, obliquely, what it is to be Scottish within this new world. Whisky became a small part of this.

The newly legal distillers weren't concerned with these wider philosophical ramifications, though. They simply wanted to sell their whiskies. Although many new distilleries opened post 1823 and consumption rose alongside exports, it was never in sufficient volume to balance the considerable increase in capacity.

AN IRISH WAKE, or the *Whisky Club, singing a Requiem to the Manes of the Persecuted and ____ Queen.*

On George IV's visit to Dublin, he called for Whisky Punch to be drunk.

Economic depression in the Highlands from the 1830s onwards, coupled with the effects of the Clearances, had a detrimental impact on Highland whiskies, while the Lowland distilleries were over-capacity, thanks to the widespread adoption of the continuous still (*see* p.52). In simple terms, Scotch wasn't popular enough.

The Scots and English were drinking whiskey from Ireland, where the major distillers had grasped the opportunities created by the 1823 Act. In 1826, the pot still at the Midleton distillery could hold 31,500 gallons, while in Dublin, John and William Jameson, George Roe, and John Power were also building big. By 1850, however, it was clear: Scotch whisky was at a crossroads. It had to look hard at its flavour, or die.

AMERICA & CANADA 1700–1920

Why did 18th-century farmers distil? Primarily because the spirit tasted good, could make them money – or be used instead of it – and, perhaps most importantly, because it had become part of their culture. They used their own crops to produce a distillation of themselves, which meant using what was to hand – the Scots and the Irish didn't just use barley for their whiskies, but wheat, oats, and rye.

The same situation confronted the farmers who settled 18th-century America and Canada. They had left their lands in Germany, Holland, Ulster, Scotland, Ireland, and England for any number of reasons, famine among them, and wished to find a new place to put down roots that were not just physical, but cultural.

These were adaptable people. If they'd arrived in the Caribbean they would have made rum – as did the Scots arriving on Canada's eastern seaboard. For the Germans and Dutch living on the banks of the Monongahela River in Pennsylvania, that meant planting rye for bread and for liquor. So famed did the latter become that the river gave its name to America's first whiskey style.

They prospered. So much so, that, when Alexander Hamilton needed to pay off his new country's $54 million debt in 1791, he chose the softest-available target for taxation – booze. The subsequent rebellion by the distillers, centred on Pittsburgh, took a militia of 15,000 to quell.

Some of the distillers had already slipped along the Ohio River into Kentucky, which was by that time being settled by Scots and Irish farmers who were making whiskey of a different style. Rye wasn't the main crop here; corn was. The hooch was sold at the farm door, bartered, and quaffed in the "ordinaries": the taverns where communities were forged.

No one knows who the first Kentuckian distiller was, but the roll-call of the late 1700s includes Elijah Pepper, Jakob Boehm (aka Jacob Beam), and Evan Williams. They fired up their small pots, or adapted logs into crude stills, and made their "bald face".

As the business grew, so the whiskey was shipped further afield in casks, specifically downstream (after the Louisiana Purchase in 1801) on the Ohio and Mississippi to New Orleans, a trip which, writer Gaz Regan points out, could have taken nine months from distillation to arrival, sufficient time for the whiskey to pick up colour and have some of its roughest edges blunted. Just as the Monongahela had given its name to a style, so Bourbon County, then covering most of northern Kentucky, gave its name to this new whiskey.

Another of our gentlemen travellers, Englishman Charles Janson, certainly didn't approve of the manner in which the locals in Virginia, the Carolinas, and Georgia eased themselves into the day in 1807. He commented:

"The European learns with astonishment that the first craving of an American, in the morning, is for ardent spirits, mixed with sugar, mint, or some other hot herb; and which are called slings."

Clearly Janson hadn't read his Johnson.

At 11am, Janson goes on disapprovingly, the drinker would have his Sling from the bar while, according to the contemporaneous *American Encyclopedia*, whiskey "curiously flavoured with apples" would be the accompaniment to the evening meal.

This sweetened, mint leaf-garnished, whiskey picker-upper is best known as a Julep, a style of drink – originally brandy-based – that probably arrived in the southern states of the US with French settlers, but became associated with whiskey when the spirit became ubiquitous, and cheaper.

To Scots, the Julep/Sling was a cold Whisky Toddy with mint added. When, in America, bitters began to be added, it became a Bittered Sling or, in the definition that appeared in the *Balance and Columbian Repository* (May 6, 1806), a cocktail (though this is not, as widely thought, the first printed reference to a cocktail).

By 1842 when Charles Dickens and Washington Irving were regaling each other with tales long into the night over "an enormous, enchanted Julep", whiskey was not only a fixture in drinking culture but was made with better base spirit.

This was thanks to the arrival at the Oscar Pepper distillery in 1824 of a young Scot called James Crow. He approached distillation in forensic detail, introducing sour-mashing, hydrometers, cut points – in short, modern quality control. As a result, bourbon gained that vital element for any spirit: consistency.

In the same year, Canada was emerging from an era of small farm production with the building, by

Thomas Molson, of a purpose-built distillery next to his family's brewery in Montreal. Throughout the 19th century, millers, mostly of English ancestry, would build the foundations of a Canadian whisky industry, occasionally using barley, but predominantly making a wheat-based, rye-accented spirit.

Canadian drinkers weren't slinging it, though. According to whisky historian Davin de Kergommeaux, they seemed to have enjoyed coloured (unaged) whisky taken off a single pass of the still, which was then diluted and, from the 1820s, filtered through charcoal.

Indeed, filtration is another factor that sets North American whiskies apart (*see* p.55). The technique was fundamental to the whiskies being made by a half-forgotten grouping, America's "rectifiers". These were brokers and merchants who bought new spirit and blended it into their own-name whiskeys. Many were reputable, helping to create the first whiskey brands, but others lived on whiskey's dark side. The responsible ones sometimes redistilled the base spirits, then filtered, blended, and coloured the result. The others simply blended together various ingredients of dubious quality and passed the result off as whiskey.

The Civil War (1860–65) devastated the smaller American distillers in the southern states. Post-war, whiskey-making became a speciality, increasingly

By the start of the 19th century, American drinkers were enjoying whiskey cocktails.

HOW TO MAKE YOUR OWN WHISKEY WITHOUT DISTILLATION

WHO NEEDS A STILL?
(*The Manufacture of Liquors, Wines and Cordials Without the Aid of Distillation*, Pierre Lacour, 1853)

Lacour hailed from Bordeaux but was based in New Orleans and, from the tone of his tome, was a fervent believer in making health-giving liquors without the tedious bother of mashbills or maturation.

"**Irish Whiskey:** Neutral spirits, four gallons; refined sugar, three pounds, in water, four quarts; creasote [sic], four drops; color with four ounces burnt sugar.

"**Scotch Whiskey [sic]** Neutral spirits, four gallons; alcoholic solution of starch, one gallon; creasote [sic], five drops; cochineal tincture, four wine glass full; burnt sugar coloring, quarter of a pint.

"**Old Bourbon Whiskey:** Neutral Spirits, four gallons; refined sugar, three pounds, dissolved in water, three quarts; decoction of tea, one pint; three drops of oil of wintergreen, dissolved in one ounce of alcohol; color with tincture of cochineal, two ounces; burnt sugar, three ounces.

"**Monongahela Whiskey:** Neutral spirit, four gallons; honey, three pints, dissolved in water, one gallon; alcoholic solution of starch, one gallon; rum, half a gallon; nitric ether, half an ounce; this is to be colored to suit fancy."

focused on Kentucky, which had survived in a slightly better condition than its neighbours, mainly because of the state's neutrality during the early part of the conflict. The industry that emerged was different in shape, size, and attention to detail. Some old-stagers, like Pepper, Beam, and Dant, survived and were now joined by newcomers like Brown-Forman, Taylor, and – in Tennessee – Jack Daniel. Barrel-ageing became commonplace – though rectifiers were still shovelling tinted harsh hooch onto the trains which, by 1869, crossed the continent.

This didn't mean that the whole of America suddenly started to drink top-end bourbon and rye. By the end of the century, upwards of 75 per cent of the whiskey being drunk there was rectified – while Canada was also establishing a foothold, having taken advantage of the shortages during the Civil War and started to export in volume. The Civil War was the making of the Canadian whisky industry; it wasn't until 2010 that American whiskey outsold Canadian in the US.

One of the (reputable) rectifiers was Detroit-based Hiram Walker, who bought a mill/distillery in Windsor, Canada, in 1858. Other new Canadian distilleries, often attached to flour mills, were also emerging, such as Henry Corby's, which started in 1959 in what was to become Corbyville. The year before in Prescott, JP Wiser, whose rye-based whiskies gave a hint to his German-American ancestry, had started distilling, while in 1878 a young fellow named Joseph Seagram bought the Hespeler & Randall distillery in Waterloo, Ontario.

Thanks to a lowering of the price of corn and imports from America, the Canadian distillers were now using it to make another style of whisky. It wasn't long before they then began to blend together their wheat, rye, and corn bases in order to make a more complex – and consistent – product. By the end of the 1880s, high-class brands such as Hiram Walker's Canadian Club and the sherried Seagram 83 demonstrated the Canadians' mastery of blending and sat alongside American brands like Old Crow, Old Taylor, and Old Forester (the first bourbon to be bottled) on the country's bars.

Use was widening. You could go to the cathouse or the barrel house and find the rectifiers' cheapest in tapped barrels dripping onto the sawdust-sprinkled floor, or drink whiskey in saloons of varying degrees of salubrity. The type and serve of whiskey you drank depended on the establishment and, though the east drank rye and the south and west drank bourbon, it would be a brave man who asked for a cocktail made with either in a dive. You would, however, make that call in the swanky saloons, clubs, and hotel bars where professional gentlemen were tending bar.

Jerry Thomas listed 22 whiskey-based mixed drinks in his 1865 *Bartenders Guide*, while at the same time Harry Johnson was calling the whiskey cocktail "without doubt one of the most popular American drinks in existence": evidence that the golden era of whiskey cocktails had started. The movement gained greater momentum when phylloxera removed Cognac from the barkeep's armoury. At its summit was the definitive American whiskey cocktail, the Manhattan.

It is easy to be dazzled by the recipes and conclude that everyone was experimenting wildly, but even during this high period, the four most popular examples of whiskey cocktails were the Sour, the Old-Fashioned, the Julep, and the Manhattan. Simple drinks all. In fact, most whiskey was still being drunk neat, with water on the side. Bourbon, rye and Canadian all had credentials, but rectified whiskies still ruled.

All was not happy, however. Although spirits consumption fell steadily from the middle of the 19th century, there was growing pressure to curb consumption further. By the turn of the 20th century that had hardened into demands for an outright ban. By 1915, 20 of America's states were dry, including Kentucky and Tennessee. At 12.01 am on January 17, 1920, the 18th Amendment took effect. The Noble Experiment was under way.

SCOTLAND & IRELAND 1850—1920

The first of the major transformations of Scotch came with the arrival of that spirit of capitalism, grain whisky. Lowland distillers needed to make more whisky at lower cost, so the arrival of Stein's and then Coffey's stills, in 1828 and 1834, respectively (*see* p.52), was the answer to their wishes. Their whiskies had always been different, thanks to the wide variety of grains used: malted and unmalted barley, wheat, oats, and rye. The new "grain" whisky took this base and made it lighter.

Although Scotch was still struggling to gain widespread appreciation, in 1853 a change in law permitting malt whiskies to be blended under bond (in warehouses before tax had been paid) gave malt distillers greater consistency and volume. The immediate consequence was the appearance of vatted malts, such as Usher's OVG (Old Vatted Glenlivet) – an amalgam of malts from different sites in Strathspey (the pre-20th-century term for Speyside). The major change occurred seven years later, when further legislation allowed the vatting of casks of grain and malt in bond, making large-scale blending commercially viable. In 1860 the Scotch industry that we now know started to emerge.

With the change in rules appeared a new class of whisky-maker: the blender. Blending liquors was not unknown – rum had been blended for the British Navy by ED&F Man from 1784, and Scottish brands, like Morton's OVD (Old Vatted Demerara), existed two decades before Usher's OVG.

The new Scotch blenders also needed to learn from their rivals' experience. As Charles Tovey outlined in 1860:

"[in England] whisky... is generally offered for sale and brought into consumption quite new from the still... spirit merchants should allow the same privilege afforded to brandy or rum that age in bond."

While far-sighted distillers and merchants had been laying down stock, maturation needed to become standard practice.

Thankfully, the Scots drank a lot of fortified wine and rum, so there were plenty of empty casks on the docksides that could be pressed into service by new whisky brokers such as Messrs Robertson & Baxter, whose lab in Glasgow became a college of blending for many major figures, and WP Lowrie, the pioneer of sherry-cask ageing and the quality control of wood.

Equally important were the grocers – or "Italian warehousemen" as the more upscale described themselves. Men like the Chivas brothers, whose King Street shop in Aberdeen would become known as "the Harrods of the North"; or John Walker, who had inherited a grocery shop in Kilmarnock in 1820. There was the Glasgow grocer William Teacher, wine merchants like Matthew Gloag and John Dewar of Perth; and George Ballantine of Edinburgh. All were selling whisky from their earliest days – in 1825, Walker had stocks of casks of "aqua" (unspecified, probably new, spirit) and Islay. By the 1860s, the Chivas brothers were selling Royal Glen Dee and Royal Strathythan, both probably vatted malts; Dewar's first blend also came in the 1860s, as did Walker's Old Highland.

These early blends were bold and rich, with heavy malts being given dilution by – often unaged – grain whisky. A house style, dictated by geography, was already emerging – roots that are still noticeable today. Walker, in Kilmarnock, based its blends on the rich and smoky whiskies of the west; the Chivas brothers sourced from Strathspey, Dewar from Perthshire.

The fact that many were grocers is significant. Blends weren't just a way of making malts more easy to drink; they were a response to a shift in the

The grand emporia of "Italian warehousemen" were the birthplace of many major Scotch blends. Pictured is the Chivas brothers' King Street shop in Aberdeen.

Late 19th-century bar manuals, such as *Bariana*, contained large numbers of whisky-based cocktails.

consumer's mind. Cookery books from the 19th century list ingredients considered exotic today. The blenders, surrounded by the scents of the world, were tapping into a changing sense of taste.

These ingredients were transported to Scotland by new shipping companies such as Jardine Mathieson, formed after the break-up of the East India Company. In came tea (to be blended by the grocers) and out went whisky (to be sold on a commission basis).

Scotch was also arriving in America. Bartender Jerry Thomas' signature Blue Blazer cocktail was Scotch-based, while his 1862 *Bartenders Guide* specifies Glenlivet or Islay whisky for his Scotch Whisky Skin and Hot Scotch Whisky Punch, while Islay is mixed with Monongahela rye for the Spread Eagle Punch, showing that it wasn't only blends that were being sold. Single malt and vatted malts would remain significant throughout the 19th century. Glen Grant was being quaffed in Sierra Leone in 1853.

From the 1860s onwards, Glenlivet (a designation covering Strathspey) was changing in flavour. As the railways entered the region, so distillers could get access to coal, reducing their dependence on peat and thereby lightening the character of their whiskies. A second wave of plants was built producing this lighter style, which had been dictated by the blenders. They were now calling the shots and doing so by looking at flavour.

By the end of the century, Sir Alexander (Alec) Walker had arranged his vast stocks by name and style – not location. His blending recipe books are simple affairs, giving percentages of these flavour blocks. Walker's current master blender, Jim Beveridge, feels this suggests that his predecessor was creating pre-blend vats defined by flavour.

The Scots blenders had to be innovative, because they were still lagging behind the Irish in terms of popularity. The 19th century was Irish whiskey's golden age, thanks to the urban distillers who inadvertently created a new style – single pot still – by adding unmalted barley to malted in order to avoid paying the malt tax. The scale of their distilleries allowed each one to produce specific characters of single pot still in volume which, whether it was sold to merchants or under their own auspices, was consistent in flavour and quality and had the maker's name on the bottle as a guarantee. As early as 1862, Jerry Thomas recommends Kinahan's and Jamieson's [sic] whiskey.

Then the Scotch blenders made a breakthrough. Instead of blending and hoping for the best, they worked out what flavour of whisky their potential drinkers wanted. It had long been known that the London palate was lighter than the Glasgow one, so blenders such as James Buchanan (Buchanan's, Black & White), James Greenlees, and Tommy Dewar crafted blends to suit.

Fortune was on their side. In 1877, phylloxera devastated the Cognac vineyards in France. In the quarter century it took for the vineyards to be replanted, Scotch and soda had usurped brandy and soda. The Highball, a British creation, was the breakthrough Scotch blends needed – and it had middle-class respectability. Not only were blends being tailored to a consumer, they were also being blended to suit being mixed.

In the 1900 edition of his *Bartenders' Manual*, New York bartender Harry Johnson lists seven blended Scotches and the same number of Scotch cocktails, while *Bariana*, published in Paris in 1896, lists 32 whisky drinks, with 22 of them specifying Scotch (or Irish). This wasn't just a neat spirit; it was still being spun into new shapes. The biggest surprise comes in William Schmidt's *The Flowing Bowl*, (1892), which includes a recipe for a French concoction called *scubac*. Our old friend usquebaugh had crossed the Channel and changed its name.

Global sales began to grow, initially thanks to the Scottish diaspora, while advertising was being successfully pioneered. In 1898, Tommy Dewar commissioned the world's first filmed advertisement, while a decade later James Stevenson – the forgotten genius behind the building of Johnnie Walker – hired an advertising agent called Paul E Derrick, who commissioned the drawing of the "striding man" logo. Scotch was no longer an odd product from a small, wet country; it had become a brand and it had done so by being mixed and drunk long.

Although World War I was a tough time for the Scotch business – with compulsory closures of malt

Embracing the new medium of advertising helped Johnnie Walker to become a global brand.

"—Born 1820
Still going strong
—1920
One hundred years"

"Thanks! same tae ye"

distilleries, tax hikes, and minimum pricing – the industry emerged in the 1920s in a better position than its two main rivals, who were about to face their biggest crises.

JAPAN

When, in 1854, Captain William Perry's black ships sailed into Yokohama Bay to force open the doors of Japan to trade, he brought some liquid emollient: whisky. On March 15, a cask of either American or Scotch (no one can confirm which) was delivered to the emperor. It was the Scots who were to become the main beneficiaries of Japan's emergence. As soon as the British signed a similar deal later that year, traders Jardine Mathieson opened a Yokohama office and Scotch and Irish whiskies began to be sold, some over the bar of the town's Grand Hotel, which boasted Japan's first Western-style cocktail bar.

The whisky links had been sealed in 1873, when the Iwakura trade delegation returned from its two-year mission to establish business connections with the West carrying a case of Old Parr. In the 1890s, a Glaswegian, Captain Albert Richard Brown, was the first person to chart Japan's coast. This was soon to be guarded by lighthouses planned by Aberdonian engineer Henry Brunton, patrolled by warships built by Thomas Blake Glover (aka The Scottish Samurai), and equipped with armaments from Glasgow factories.

These links meant that most major Scotch blends were soon available in Japan. In 1907, James Buchanan & Co was granted a royal warrant by the emperor. Its Royal Household blend is still a Japanese exclusive. Meanwhile, the flavours of Western-style spirits (*yo-shu*) were being fabricated by various firms which added flavourings, spices, and essences to a base spirit – in much the same way as American rectifiers. The Nonjatta blog on Japanese whisky has an entertaining account of American troops being sideswiped after overenthusiastic consumption of a Japanese *yo-shu* whisky called Queen George when on shore leave in Hokkaido in 1918.

It was Japanese-distilled whisky, not *yo-shu*, that was the dream of the young Shinjiro Torii and, by 1919, he had plans to make his vision a reality. He was not alone.

TWO *SCUBACS*

IRISH *SCUBAC*
(*The Wine and Spirit Merchants Own Book*, CC Dornat, 1855)

Extra Fine "The zests of 4 lemons, angelica seed, coriander and green anise, 4 drachms of each; cinnamon 9 drachms; mace and cloves 2 drachms; pound and infuse in 6 quarts of alcohol for 5 days then distil in a water bath. Boil in the water jujube, dates, and malaga raisins, 4 drachms of each having stoned them, squeeze them and mix the juice to the products of distillation, add 24 drops of essence of neroli and let the whole thing stand a fortnight before filtering."

Irish Usquebaugh, which the French call *Scubac* (*The Flowing Bowl*, "The Only William" (aka W Schmidt), 1892)

"This famous cordial, which the French call *Scubac*, is prepared in various ways. One and one-fifth ounces of nutmeg, as much of cloves and of cinnamon, two and one-third ounces of anise, as much of kummel and coriander are mashed; put this with four ounces of licorice root, twenty-three quarts of rectified alcohol, and four and a half quarts of water in the distilling apparatus; color the condensed liquor with saffron, and sweeten with sugar syrup."

Masataka Taketsuru (here with his Scottish wife, Rita) was one of the founding fathers of Japanese whisky.

The year before, a young man from Hiroshima, Masataka Taketsuru, had been sent to Glasgow by his employer Settsu Shizo to learn the science of whisky-making. In 1920, after working at a number of distilleries, Taketsuru returned home (with a Scottish wife) only to discover that financial problems had put paid to any hope of Settsu Shizo investing in a distillery.

By then, however, Torii had bought a plot of land at Yamazaki, close to Kyoto. Taketsuru was the obvious choice as manager and, in 1929, Torii's firm (today called Suntory) launched Japan's first domestic whisky blend, Shiro Fuda (White Label). Too heavy and smoky for the Japanese palate, it flopped. Soon after, Taketsuru left to start his own company – now called Nikka – in Hokkaido.

Torii understood that Japanese whisky had to match Japanese sensibilities. It should be light, suited to being drunk with food, and be poured as a refreshing serve to slake thirsts in the humid summers. It had to chime with a cultural aesthetic. In 1937 his solution, Kakubin, was launched. It remains Japan's top-selling blend.

Japanese whisky had to wait until after 1945 to gain true momentum, initially by satisfying the liquor needs of the country's American occupiers. But, as the economy gained in strength, whisky of all types became a liquid symbol for the new Japan.

In 1952, Torii founded a chain of bars, called Tory's, to help promote his whiskies, while the next two decades saw other firms building new distilleries (Hombu, Karuizawa, Shirakawa, Kawasaki) and the arrival of brands such as Ocean, King, and Nikka's Black. This boom was driven by the creation of a new serve, the Mizuwari. It's not complicated: tall glass, whisky, ice, lots of cold water, 3½ stirs. Torii's philosophy was being proved correct. Mizuwari allowed whisky to be drunk with food – and in quantity. It was the salaryman's fuel.

The Mizuwari generations helped Japanese – and imported – whisky to enjoy almost four decades of boom times. New distilleries, like Miyagikyo and Hakushu, were built: the latter for a time the largest malt distillery in the world. In the 1980s Suntory Old was selling 12.4 million cases a year in Japan alone.

Then, in 1991, Japan's "bubble economy" burst, ushering in two decades of stagnation in blended whisky sales. Whisky became the drink of the past, the drink of old men, the fathers' and grandfathers' drink. Distilleries closed, brands were rationalized. And yet Japan's reputation rose among whisky-lovers. Its long love affair with all whiskies and a Japanese obsessive attention to detail had resulted in its bars becoming the greatest repositories of whisky in the world, its bartenders the guardians of classical bartending techniques. Whisky-lovers began to travel to worship at these dimly lit shrines.

The upside of the decline was that, for the first time, Japan's distillers needed to export – and did so with single malt. Immediately it was hailed as a classic style. It was a glimmer of hope. Then, at the start of the millennium, Japanese whisky began to rise once more domestically – its salvation coming from an unlikely serve, the Highball.

WHISKY 1920—2000

It's untrue that America went on a drunken binge during Prohibition. By 1929, total consumption was lower than in 1915, when states began to dry up. What had happened was a switch by the American drinker from beer to spirits, arresting a 75-year decline. By 1922, illicit stills along the Appalachians were running hot to meet demand. By the late twenties, a web of "alky cookers" had emerged in city tenements, using supplies from a corn-sugar industry that had mysteriously expanded from selling 152,000 lb a year in 1921, to close to 1,000,000 lb. For a 50¢ outlay, the moonshiner could sell a gallon of hooch to the distributor for $2, who would then sell it in a speakeasy for 25¢ a shot (or $40 a gall). Moonshine was easy – and big – money.

Industrial alcohol was also being diverted and doctored. Just like the less reputable 19th-century rectifiers, the bootleggers would make "Scotch" by throwing in some caramel, prune juice and, depending on how smoky the discerning punters wished their "Scotch" to be, creosote.

Imported Scotch was also flowing through America's porous borders. In an attempt to ensure that the reputation of its Scotch brands were not sullied, the largest player, DCL, attempted to control the "Special

Despite the efforts of Prohibition agents, whisky sales grew during the Noble Experiment.

Prohibition-era speakeasies saw an increase in spirit-drinking – and in female customers.

Trade" by grading brands into first and second class, and only supplying the top grade if the second-class brands were also ordered. The firm also controlled prices and vetted "importers" in an attempt to keep Scotch out of the clutches of the gangs.

Though they shipped whiskies to America, Canadian importers like Henry Hatch and Sam Bronfman were not considered bootleggers. Hatch had purchased Gooderham & Worts in 1923 and, by 1926, had taken over Hiram Walker. "Hatch's Navy" sailed nightly across Lake Ontario with cargoes of his whiskies.

Sam Bronfman started with his brother Harry in 1923 as a blender, broker, and distributor of DCL brands. The brothers also ran liquor cross-border. When the Bronfmans made a de facto takeover of Seagram in 1928, one of the most powerful spirits empires of the 20th century was founded. Hatch and Bronfman weren't doing anything illegal as far as the Canadian authorities were concerned. All they required was for the duties to be paid in Canada.

Irish was the only imported style missing from the Prohibition party. Ireland had spent the early part of the twenties building itself to an independent country, albeit one without a whiskey industry. The new government in the republic, desperate for revenue, taxed whiskey to the hilt and with export to the British Empire cut off, distilleries foundered. Joe Kennedy (father of JFK) visited Dublin in the 1920s to try and get Jameson and Power to sign a distribution agreement for America, but they refused to enter into a business deal they considered illegal. America, their last hope, was cut off, allowing Scotch to clean up. Perhaps surprisingly, despite its geographical proximity, Canadian whisky didn't increase its sales as dramatically as Scotch during Prohibition.

Times were good. By 1929, it was estimated that New York City had twice as many speakeasies as it had legal saloons a decade before. Behind the peepholes drinkers' behaviour was changing. In those high times the people were carousing on bootleg booze, reefer, and cocaine. Or at least the well-heeled were. With drink prices rising tenfold, only they could afford the speakeasy life, drinking in hedonistic, decadent shrines to a new age where drunkenness was worn as a badge of honour.

A new world seemed to be taking shape, with jazz as its soundtrack – the percussive rattle of ice in the shaker its rhythm section, and a descant (for the first time in licensed premises) provided by the laughter of paying women customers. The Prohibition era in America saw the first emergence of a rebellious, youth-oriented culture. It was a time of possibilities – if you had the cash. If you didn't there was always the hooch boiled up by the "alky cookers".

At home, the Scotch industry was rationalizing, the most significant event being the merger in 1925 of DCL with the three major blenders: Buchanan, Dewar, and Walker. Not that this bothered the Bright Young Things quaffing drinks in fashionable nightclubs in London and Paris, where blended Scotch was being experimented with. In 1933, Harry Craddock's *The Savoy Cocktail Book* lists 45 Scotch drinks and 40 using Canadian rye. In 1937, London's Café Royal had 33 Scotch drinks, the same number of bourbon, and

Featuring cocktail recipes compiled by legendary bartender Harry Craddock, 1930's *The Savoy Cocktail Book* is a repository of many whisky drinks.

34 with Canadian. Scotch was egalitarian – drunk neat but more often as a Highball, and in mixed drinks.

Repeal coincided with America being in the middle of the Great Depression. Unsurprisingly, many former distillers looked at the wasteland and walked away. Of the brave who restarted, some had whisky in their veins like the Beam, Samuels, and Brown families. Others, like the Shapiras of Heaven Hill, had vision. All had to start from nothing and, in the hiatus between restarting and releasing whiskey, Scotch was stealing ever more of the market while the big Canadian players were moving in. At its height, Seagram owned 13 distilleries in America, including Four Roses, which it bought in 1943.

Just as the American industry had staggered to its feet, along came World War II and whiskey-making was shut down again. Across the Atlantic, however, the UK government commanded the Scotch industry to export. On average, three million gallons of Scotch a year were shipped to America during the war. Post-war, this export-focused strategy continued. In 1945, Winston Churchill said:

> "On no account reduce the barley for whisky. This takes years to mature and is an invaluable export and dollar producer."

Blends not only saved Scotch whisky; they helped the nation's recovery.

Thankfully America wanted Scotch, even if its palate had changed since Prohibition. Rye had gone, straight bourbon was struggling. The demand was for liquor that was clean and light: American blends like 7 Crown; Canadian blends like Canadian Club or Crown Royal; and Scotches like Cutty Sark – created for Berry Bros in 1923 by a blender for hire, Charles H Julian. In 1933 he performed the same task for wine merchant Justerini & Brooks, reformulating its brand into the J&B Rare we know today.

They, along with the brands that had built their reputations through Prohibition and the War (Peter Dawson, Dewar's, and Walker Red especially) grew quickly, and in 1954 they were joined by Chivas Regal 12 year old, blended for Sam Bronfman by... Charles H Julian. Blended Scotch was nothing if not adaptable. As a result, it ruled America – with a dash of soda.

Brands such as Cutty Sark were created to suit the lighter American palate.

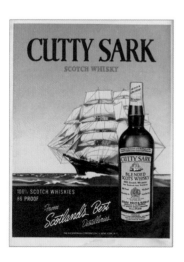

Those crazy days of speaking free while pumped on hard liquor had long gone. In the fifties, America got serious and concentrated on its economy. By then, though, Scotch had acquired a reputation for being an awkward customer in the realm of mixed drinks – a reputation it has found hard to shake off.

In 1958, that great analyser of mixed drinks, David Embury, felt that:

"On account of their pronounced smoky taste, most Scotches are not as adaptable to cocktail-making as rye or bourbon. They should be taken straight or as a Highball... [though] just how the fetish or superstition that Scotch and soda is the gentleman's drink and that American whiskies are plebeian and inferior [occurred] would be hard to determine."

He was correct in one way. Scotch may have won, but in doing so it had transformed itself into a safe, "gentlemanly" drink, and one that was becoming prematurely middle-aged. Scotch may have been mixed, but it was undeniably straight.

The last glimpse of Scotch as an edgy spirit comes in the pages of Ian Fleming's *James Bond*. Bond's favourite drink wasn't the Martini, but Scotch and soda. *Thunderball*'s plot is predicated on his hangover after drinking 11 of them. When it came to translating Bond onto screen in the 1960s, however, the urbane secret agent was sipping white spirits, a sign of how Scotch's image was shifting.

On one hand, blended Scotch remained the default drink of the managerial class, but as the sixties moved into the seventies it had also become shorthand for the depressed or untrustworthy. J R Ewing drank whiskey, Bobby Ewing didn't. In country and blues music, whiskey had become the amber refuge of the lost, heartbroken, and bitter. Willie Nelson sings:

"Whiskey river take my mind, don't let her memory torture me. Whiskey river don't run dry, you're all I've got to take care of me."

Good song, but hardly one to promote the drink.

Hippies didn't drink whisky, even though rock stars needing to cultivate a rebel image would immediately stretch a hand around the neck of a square bottle from Tennessee. Scotch, meanwhile, was becoming complacent and, as it did so, vodka, that perfect post-modernist spirit, that triumph of surface over depth, the drink that sees no flavour as being a positive attribute, took control.

By the end of the 1970s, sales were slipping in Scotch's main markets, but its sales departments refused to believe the facts. Production remained high even as drinkers rejected their father's drink. A whisky loch formed and began to deepen. By 1982, rationalization was needed and when it came it was brutal, with mass closures of distilleries.

As so often, at this low point there were indications that whisky was once again changing itself to rise above a crisis. The answer, this time, didn't come from blends but from single malt. Though these had been sold since the 19th century, it was only from the late 1970s onwards that they began to be marketed. Glenfiddich, The Glenlivet, The Macallan, Glen Grant, and then Diageo's six-strong Classic Malts changed whisky's landscape. Single malt told a new whisky story, one of provenance, history, place, and intensity of flavour – and one to be taken with only a splash of water, if that. The era of neat whisky had arrived.

Malt whisky ushered in an era of big flavour, a trend that didn't go unnoticed by bourbon producers. A new wave of big-boned, flavour-packed, premium bourbons emerged. The stage was set for whisky's latest and perhaps most surprising transformation.

WHISKY TODAY

It was a combination of economics and youthful enthusiasm that did it, starting in post-Franco Spain, where a new generation (also) behaved in a patricidal manner, killing off their father's brandy and embracing blended Scotch, drunk long with cola. Though considered too outré a serve for mature markets, the Spanish phenomenon has since been picked up by post-Communist Russia, democratized South Africa, and economically vibrant Brazil, Venezuela, and China.

In each of these massive new markets, Scotch whisky is a signifier of success and was being drunk in different ways: in Brazil with coconut water, in South Africa with cola or Appletise, in China with green tea, in Russia with cola. Blends are once again the right flavour for the right occasion. Even Japan has seen young people drinking whisky again by rediscovering an old serve – the Highball. Whisky has never been a drink only ever drunk neat. Rather, it has constantly transformed to mould itself to the drinker's requirements.

At the same time, in mature markets the shift to single malts has continued, and with it has come bourbon, rye, a newly resurgent Irish category and, most recently, a reborn Canadian industry.

A generation of drinkers whose parents had rejected whisky of all kinds are now discovering it, and they have no hang-ups about how it should be drunk, mixed, or made. The start of the new millennium has not only seen the greatest increase in sales of whisky ever, it has seen its production spread around the world to every country in Europe, to Australia, Taiwan, South Africa and, most remarkably, into 200-plus craft distilleries in America. They all make whisky to suit their place, not by copying, but by making it their own.

A new generation of craft distillers (here at King's County, Brooklyn) has taken the American whiskey scene by storm.

WHISKY: THE ESSENTIALS

Whisky has never been easy. Even at its most sophisticated, it delivers the *sgailc* (a blow to the head). It is compelling, it has edge, attitude, and flavour. It can be luxury, it can be two fingers of liquor in a dirty glass, but it will never be bland. As you read this, all around the world people are sitting in circles with a bottle and glasses, talking and bonding over this liquid. It was always thus.

In the 1970s, the British punk fanzine *Sniffin' Glue* carried the following instructions: "Here are two chords. Learn them. Now form a band."

Whisky can be reduced to similar fundamentals. Make some beer. Boil it in a copper kettle. Put it into a cask. Leave it. Drink it.

Obviously, there is more to the process than that but, at its simplest, that is what whisky-makers have been doing for hundreds of years. It is how each of these distillers takes this formula and then puts his or her own individual spin on things that makes whisky such a fascinating subject.

This is not a manual of whisky-making techniques – it is one of whisky flavour and enjoyment. But to understand this globe-spanning spirit you need a basic understanding of how the fusion of the elements of earth (grain and peat), water, fire (distillation), and air (maturation) work together in alchemical congress to produce a drink with a dazzling multiplicity of flavours, characters, and styles. Understanding the flavours gives you, the drinker, a head start on knowing how best to enjoy the whisky in front of you.

GRAINS

Whisky is a cereal-based, spirit, but that is only a small part of the reality. Each cereal used – and the variety is growing every day – contributes flavour and texture to a whisky. A seed of barley or rye, or a kernel of corn might not be much to look at, but it is remarkable how they can be transformed into bread and food – it is reckoned that beer-making came as a by-product of bread-making in Sumerian times. Over the centuries, whisky-distilling has been stopped (or banned) because of the importance of cereals. They satisfy our appetites and when brewed or distilled make people happy.

All cereals are packages of starch. What a distiller needs to do is get access to that starch and transform it into a sugar-rich solution, which happens either by mixing ground cereal with hot water in a mash tun, or by cooking the grains.

It is only once that sugary liquid is created that the distiller can then add yeast and make alcohol. So how

The first stage in whisky-making is getting access to the starch in the grain – here, by mashing.

BLENDED WHISKY

Blended whisky is a carefully created amalgamation of grain whisky (a high-strength, light-flavoured spirit based on corn and/or wheat) and richer, flavoursome whiskies. In Scotland and Japan the latter will be malt whiskies; in Ireland both malt and single pot still are used; in Canada they are most commonly made from rye.

does that conversion happen? Through the work of enzymes within the cereal that have been activated through a process called malting.

Barley

Barley is the common factor in virtually all of the world's whisky styles, predominantly because it is a grain type rich in enzymes and easy to malt. This process involves fooling the barley into thinking it is time to grow by steeping it in water. The barley seed then starts to grow, or germinate. At this point, it is ready to start converting its starch into the sugars that will act as the fuse to drive the green shoot. Before that happens, this growth is stopped (see Smoke, p.46) with all the starch intact.

The distiller can then grind it up and add hot water, which triggers the enzymes into action and completes the conversion from starch to fermentable sugars.

Single-malt whisky is made exclusively from malted barley, and the most obvious flavour that comes from the grain itself is a crisp cereal note, often picked up as a background note but more overt in brands such as Knockando or Blair Athol.

Single pot still Irish whiskeys (like Redbreast or Green Spot) are made from a mixture of malted and unmalted barley, the former helping to convert the starch into sugar, the latter giving an oily, spicy, appley-blackcurrant note. Malted barley is also used for its enzymes in the making of grain whisky in Scotland, Ireland, and Japan; bourbon, rye, and Canadian whiskies.

Corn

This is the base for, unsurprisingly, corn whisky as well as all straight bourbon and Tennessee whiskeys, where it must make up a minimum of 51 per cent of the mix of cereals (aka the mashbill), and is the most commonly used cereal for the base whiskies at the heart of Canadian blends. It is also used for grain whiskies in Ireland, Japan, and (occasionally) Scotland.

The corn is first cooked to soften the starch – in the same way as a potato goes soft when you boil it – then other cereals, if used, and malted barley are added to convert the starch to sugar. Corn spirit is a fat, sweet distillate whose aromas of hot popcorn, buttered sweetcorn, and nachos immediately make you think of counting calories.

Because each grain has its own flavour, the more corn there is in the mashbill, the fatter and sweeter the whisky will be. Conversely, the more rye there is the more bite it will have. So, by varying the proportions of corn and rye (or wheat) in the mashbill, the distiller can create flavour even at this early stage of the process.

Wheat
Most Scottish grain whisky these days is made with wheat, yet it is often overlooked as a significant grain. It is also widely used in Canada – it was the base for the country's first commercial brands and these days is used as a flavouring whisky and, by Highwood, as a base whisky.

A number of straight bourbons, including Maker's Mark, WL Weller, and Old Fitzgerald, use wheat as an alternative to rye, while Bernheim Wheat is a straight version made from a minimum 51 per cent wheat. Less "fat" than corn in flavour, wheat adds delicacy, a floral sweetness, and a slightly tight finish.

Rye
You cannot ignore the manner in which rye makes its presence known in a whisky. This is not a cereal that is shy about coming forward. If you've ever taken a swig of bourbon and wondered why, halfway in, the flavours shift to something with intense, crackling spices and a mouth-awakening acidity, now you know that's rye bellowing "HOWDY!"

It was the first grain cereal that was widely used in America and, after a 70-year decline, straight rye is making a comeback, thanks to a growing demand for flavoursome whiskies. Those straight ryes (such as Sazerac, Rittenhouse, and Old Overholt) must use no less than 51 per cent of the grain in the mashbill. There are some 100 per cent examples (such as Old Potrero and Alberta Premium) that use malted rye, while it is also used as a flavouring spirit for Canadian whiskies and, occasionally, (Alberta Distillers again) as a base whisky.

A wide variety of cereals are used to make whisky.

Other Grains

Oats were widely used in Scotland up until the 18th century and in Ireland into the 20th. Some distillers in Germany, Austria, and America (including High West, Koval, and Buffalo Trace) are looking at oats afresh. These grains give a clean, slightly bitter note with real creaminess – think of porridge!

Buckwheat (technically a grass, but permitted) was used in Scotland in the 18th and 19th centuries, but today the best-known example comes from Brittany (Eddu) where it gives a highly aromatic, spicy attack akin to rye.

Triticale is a cross between rye and wheat, which is sometimes used in Canada. The flavour is, perhaps not surprisingly, halfway between the two.

Millet gives a nuttiness; but according to alternative-grain guru Darek Bell of Corsair distillery in Nashville, it is so smooth that "old-timers believed that it made a superior moonshine".

Spelt Bell has also experimented with this low-gluten grain and has found that it has a firmer and more nutty character than millet.

Quinoa As far as I know at the time of writing, Corsair is the only distillery examining this grain, which Bell says, "adds an earthy and nutty flavour to the whiskey".

SMOKE

Whisky is about flavour, and whisky-distilling is about the way in which each distiller or blender, no matter where they are in the world, creates and crafts the specific flavours that make their whisky unique. The choice of which grain types to use is the starting point on this path. A second option is whether to make the whisky smoky or not, and it is one that is taken up by single-malt producers globally. It is not compulsory; it is a flavour option.

This smokiness is introduced right at the start of the process, when the malted barley needs to be dried. The source of the smoke has its own flavour. That source is peat: partially decomposed vegetation laid down over thousands of years in bogs. Because there's not sufficient oxygen to feed the microbes that would normally break down the organic material, the plants

Lighting a fire when drying barley imparts a smoky character to the end whisky.

have not degraded totally but rotted to form the slowly thickening peat banks. When it is cut and dried it can be used as an alternative to coal.

As there is no coal in the Scottish Highlands and Islands, in the days before the railways reached the Highlands, peat was the only fuel that distillers could use to dry their malt, and so their whiskies were smoky. Smoke has remained a signature flavour of island malts – but that's not to say they are all automatically smoky.

Smokiness does not come from water, but from the burning of the peat. Its smoke contains oils called phenols, and it is these that stick to the husk of the damp barley, flavouring it. The more smoke that is burned in the kilning process, the smokier the end whiskies will be.

Think back for a second. Peat is composed of vegetation that grew on that spot up to 5,000 years ago. It might look like black mud, but it is instead a repository of flavours. Smell Highland Park and you get heather, moor burn, gentian, and an aromatic intensity to the smokiness. Is it a coincidence that the Orkney peat used in Highland Park is composed almost entirely of heather? Islay's smokiness has a certain tarry, medicinal, seashore element that could be rooted in the marine vegetation within the peat. On the mainland,

47

Plentiful water made Bushmills a noted site for mills – and a whiskey distillery.

where the peat has more wood, the aromas are more smoky, reminiscent of woodland bonfires.

Neither is peat restricted to Scotland. It was widely used in Ireland – and has been revived in Cooley's Connemara brand. Peaty whiskies are made in Japan, though these days only one distiller, Chichibu, is using local peat. In Tasmania the specific flora in that island's peat adds a scented, exotic, smoky aroma to whiskies such as Lark. The fact that there is peat throughout northern Europe, and even some in Africa (Congo and Rwanda), means that there are plenty of opportunities for new aromas in the future.

Peat is not the only source used, however. An option being explored by American craft distillers involves not just looking for smokiness – because it's a flavour people like – but for smokes that define their whiskies as American. Maybe unsurprisingly among many woods being experimented with, it is mesquite that is becoming a defining aroma of the new American whiskey frontier.

WATER

You can't make whisky from dry cereal, so water needs to be added. Hot water to be precise. This does two things. It cooks the cereal, liquidizing the starch, and also activates the enzymes within the malted barley, which then spring into action and convert this mass of starch into sugar.

Distillers put great store by their water source. They need a lot of it and they need it to be pure and free from anything that could contaminate the whisky. That is one reason why each distillery has its own source.

The creation of a whisky's flavour is the result of a myriad of different elements, all of which are interrelated. Water will not impart a massive amount of flavour to the final spirit, but the mineral composition of the water will have an impact on how effectively the yeast acts upon the wort – the sweet liquid that's been created in mashing.

Soft water – the most common source in Scotland – isn't superior to hard, which typifies the water from Kentucky and Tennessee, although using hard water has an effect on fermentation (*see* opposite).

Water is also used at the end of the distillation process when cold water is run through the condenser, turning the alcohol vapour back into liquid. Again, a lot is needed.

YEAST

So far flavour has come from the cereal types used and from whether smokiness has been imparted. The creation of most of whisky's flavours comes in the next stage: fermentation. This is achieved by adding yeast to the wort. Yeast gobbles up sugar and converts it into alcohol, CO_2, and heat – and incidentally changes the wort's name to wash.

Yet "alcohol" is too simplistic a term to use here. What the yeast actually does is create a vast range of different flavours. In simple terms, the longer the wash sits in the fermenter, the more fruity it becomes. Understanding what flavours are created at different times helps distillers create the specific ones they need.

Kentucky and Tennessee's hard water lowers the acidity of the wort, making it more difficult for the yeast to get to work. To get around this all the distillers in those states add the acidic liquid left in the still after distillation (sourmash) to their fermenters.

The yeast type used will have an impact as well. Because Scottish distillers all use the same yeast type, it doesn't create the flavours that make each distillery's whisky different. Everywhere else, however, yeast is seen as a significant contributor to flavour. Distillers will use strains unique to their distillery, maybe even to each mashbill. Four Roses distillery in Kentucky, for example, has two mashbills and five different yeast strains giving them 10 highly individual base spirits that are aged separately and then blended.

COPPER

Distillation is what separates beer from whisky. At the end of fermentation, the distiller contains a wash made up of 9% alcohol by volume (ABV) and 91 per cent water. At the end of distillation, however, the strength of the spirit will be upwards of 60% ABV. Because alcohol boils at a lower temperature than water (78.5°C/173.3°F

Many of a whisky's flavours are created during fermentation.

compared to 100°C/212°F) it is turned into vapour before water. At the end of distillation, much of the water has been separated from the alcohol. More importantly, the flavours created so far in the process are no longer in a dilute watery solution, but have been concentrated.

This magical process takes place in copper vessels called stills. It is here where the distiller makes the decision as to which of the flavours he wishes to keep to make his signature spirit – and which he wishes to discard. Copper is his faithful assistant in this.

The properties of copper are many, but it is what it can do during distillation that is the most remarkable. Copper holds on to heavy elements within the alcohol vapours that are rising up the body of the still. The longer the conversation is between the copper and the vapour, the lighter the resulting spirit will be. So, a tall still will be likely to give lighter characters compared to a small still. The shape of a still is therefore vitally important in the creation of the final flavour.

There are two types of stills.

Pot Stills

Any of the early alchemists cracking the distillation code would recognize the shape of today's pot stills which, though larger and more refined in terms of additions and condensing systems, perform an identical function. Their name hints at their use in the period of the smuggling era when they would have innocently doubled up as large copper cooking vessels.

In pot-still distillation, the wash is placed in the body of the still. As heat is applied, so the alcohol vapour is released, rising over the neck of the still and into a condensing system. In its oldest form, the worm tub (the pipe containing the vapour) is permanently immersed in a large tank of cold water. When the hot vapour meets the cold surface of the pipe it turns back into liquid once again. Not only has the flavour been intensified and the strength increased, but the muddy colour of the wash has been removed. Seeing new spirit trickling from a still you immediately understand why it was called "the water of life". The strength of these "low wines" is around 23% ABV, but as there are still unwanted flavours in there, the

The stillhouse at Caol Ila distillery on Islay is one of the most spectacular in the world.

process is repeated, which increases the strength and lightens the character. In single pot still Irish whiskey and some single malts (Bushmills, Auchentoshan, and Hazelburn) a third distillation will take place, lightening the spirit further.

During this final run, the distiller makes a decision as to what flavours he wishes to retain for ageing in cask. The first vapours to be condensed are too strong and potent and are diverted into a holding vessel. The oily, greasy liquid that comes across at the very end is also unwanted and is run into the same holding tank.

In the middle, however, is clean spirit with a range of flavours to choose from. It isn't just ethanol that is coming across, but also a host of different flavour compounds, each of which has a different weight.

The lightest – which have the most delicate aromas – appear first; the heaviest – such as smoke – tarry towards the end. By knowing which flavours appear at what point the distiller can take a slice from whatever part of this "middle cut" he wishes to – but it will be the same cut every time.

If he wants light then he'll concentrate on the aromas of flowers and grasses at the front end; if he wants fruits then a cut into the centre will be more desirable; if it's lots of smoke he's after then he might pass on the light elements and concentrate on the later aromas. Each distiller has his own recipe. The stuff in the holding tank? It's mixed with the next lot of low wines and redistilled.

Column Stills

Pot-still distillation is a stop–start process. You have to take your liquid, boil it up, collect it, put it back into another still, boil it again, separate it into three, collect some and recycle the rest. So, when whisky was becoming an industry and distillers had a commercial gleam in their eyes, the call went out to create a still that would be capable of producing large volumes of spirit in a more efficient manner. Wouldn't it be great, distillers said, to have a still where as long as wash was fed in one end you would get spirit flowing out of the other?

Across Europe, many attempts were made to design a continuous still. In whisky, a Lowland Scot distiller, Robert Stein, patented his own design in 1827, which was then refined by Irishman Aeneas Coffey in 1834. It is Coffey's design that continues to be used globally for the production of grain (or base) whisky.

What Coffey did was separate the functions of a pot still into two very tall columns, both filled with live steam. One was where the alcohol was stripped off and turned into vapour. This would then be carried by a pipe to the base of the second column where it was released and allowed to rise. This column was separated horizontally into compartments by perforated trays. Only the very lightest of flavour compounds were able to rise to the top of the column and be collected as spirit.

The same principle of flavour selection can be applied here as well. Rather than cutting the spirit into three parts, here the distiller knows what flavours exist at which points in this second column – each compartment will have a different character. This means he can decide where to draw the vapour off and condense it into spirit. Because of the height of the columns, the spirit was not only significantly stronger – 94% ABV, compared to 70% ABV – but much more delicate in character.

In bourbon production the first distillation takes place in a tall "beer still".

Combinations

Bourbon distillers use a mixture of the two still types. A single column still, known as the beer still, strips off the alcohol and starts the separation of flavours. The liquid residue at the bottom of the beer still is the sourmash used during fermentation. A second distillation then takes place in a pot still known as a doubler.

As with any distillation, the higher the strength of the final spirit, the lighter its character will be, which means that a full-blooded bourbon like Wild Turkey is collected at a lower strength compared to a light one like Maker's Mark. Again, it's up to each distiller.

OAK

Although some whiskies are bottled fresh from the still (corn whiskey does not need to be aged) and there is a (worrying, I believe) trend towards "white whiskies" in America, maturation is a defined and compulsory element in the production of the vast majority of whiskies. Scotch and Irish, for example, have to be three years of age before they can be called whisky. Legally, the period of maturation for virtually all whisky styles must take place in oak casks: new charred ones in the case of bourbon, rye, and Tennessee whiskies. For me, if there is no maturation, then the spirit isn't whisky; it's a sort of vodka.

This is not wasted time. Up to 70 per cent of a whisky's flavour comes from the interaction between the cask and the spirit.

Three things happen during maturation. The first is the removal of the harsh elements in the new spirit that make even the most hardened drinker wince. These either evaporate, or are absorbed by the charcoal layer on the inside of the cask.

At the same time, the cask is talking to the spirit. A cask isn't (or shouldn't be) an inert vessel. It's an active participant in flavour creation, a reservoir of aroma, colour, and tannin, which helps give mouthfeel. All of these are being absorbed into the spirit.

Once there they start their own dance with the flavours created by the distiller and over time new aromas are created. It is not something that can be rushed.

Bourbon and Tennessee whiskeys can only be matured in new casks, but all other styles will reuse casks. Because the spirit pulls flavour from the wood, the first time a cask is filled there will be more to be absorbed. With each subsequent fill there will be less flavour in the oak. As long as this is monitored – there's no use in putting whisky into a dead cask – the distiller can create subtly different variations on the original character. A whisky aged for 10 years in a fresh cask will taste different to the same whisky aged in a reused cask.

The species of oak used also has an impact on flavour. **American oak** is used initially by the bourbon industry and then reused by Scottish, Canadian, Irish, and Japanese distillers. This gives aromas of vanilla, coconut, cherry, pine, sweet spice, and tobacco. **European oak** casks used in the sherry industry are then pressed into service by the Scots, Irish, Canadians, and Japanese. It has more mouth-drying tannin, a mahogany colour and aromas of dried fruit, clove, and resin. **French oak** has a more pronounced spiciness. **Japanese oak,** currently only used in that country, gives an aroma akin to incense and adds greater levels of acidity to the end product.

By mixing casks that have been filled a different number of times and using different oak types, a complex web of flavours can be created around the original spirit.

Different fills of casks will result in different flavours within the whisky.

FILTRATION

Burned wood (*i.e.* charcoal) has been used in whiskey-making in North America since 1810 and is the process that separates Tennessee whiskey from bourbon. Dripping the new spirit through vats of maple charcoal helps to remove harshness and aggression from the new spirit before it goes into cask.

The other element is time. The oak will always eventually dominate the spirit. A distiller doesn't want that; he is looking for balance and harmony. An older whisky is therefore not automatically a better one, it is just an older one. Age is not a determinant of quality.

PEOPLE

The more you enjoy whisky, and as its flavours work their way into your psyche, the more you want to discover its ultimate secret, the magic formula that creates such a fascinating, complex drink. Yet, every whisky-lover and whisky-maker eventually accepts that no one will ever know everything and that in fact there is no magic formula. The enjoyment of flavour is all that matters.

Whisky is not some technological creation; it is a human one. People make this spirit, not machines. People who have handed down the art of taking a cereal and transforming it into something potent, flavoursome, and enjoyable. They are there in every part of the process: throwing the barley, adding the yeast, understanding the smells, hisses, and creaks of the distillery, caring for the casks in the crepuscular silence of a warehouse. They are men and women with whisky in their blood, whose parents and grandparents worked in the distillery before them – people for whom whisky-making is an intuitive art.

There are also whisky-makers with PhDs in biochemistry, but they, too, would reject the notion that all they are doing is applying their scientific knowledge. They understand that whisky-making is a creative act. They're the people who control the flavours of whisky. They are the blenders.

BLENDING

We all encounter blends regularly. Champagne is a blended wine, as are the great wines from Bordeaux. Tea and coffee are blended, so are perfumes and cigars. Few people seem concerned that Cognac is a blended spirit yet, when it comes to whisky, in Europe and North America blends are considered – wrongly – to be inferior to single malts. They aren't.

Since 92 per cent of the Scotch whisky sold in the world is blended, you could argue that 90 per cent of consumers are drinking blends – that's 82 million cases a year. Add in Japanese, Canadian, and Irish blends and then ask yourself: are all of these people deluded fools, or might they be on to something? Even single malt and straight bourbon are made by mingling together casks to produce a consistent flavour – they're blended.

Scotch Blends

In simple terms, a blended Scotch is a mixture of grain whisky and single malt – usually plural in both cases. It is a three-dimensional process where flavours don't simply add up A+B+C but in a cumulative fashion where the amalgamation of ingredients produces something new and greater than the sum of its parts.

Blenders work out how one whisky gives aromatic lift, another some smokiness; or the way in which one aged in sherry casks gives grip and texture, one aged in American oak provides vanilla and coconut, and one aged in refill casks gives vibrancy. The key isn't just throwing different flavours and textures together, but having an understanding of how these apparently disparate elements work in harmony with each other.

Grain whisky (*see* p.52) is important to this. It, rather than malts, are the real heart of a blend. Grain whisky adds its light flavour – often enhanced by ageing in fresh American oak – but just as importantly it adds silkiness of mouthfeel and has the ability to bind together the more intense malts and allow their hidden elements to come to the fore. Grain holds, lengthens, reveals, and creates new flavours.

There is a tendency to view the malt component of a blend as being comprised of the single malts we know as bottled brands, but this is rarely the case. You need to change your perspective regarding malt when you encounter blending and think not of the distillery but of the disparate flavours being used as building blocks.

The key is balance. Even the lightest blends – Cutty Sark, for example – will need some heavy sherried malts in the mix to act as an anchor. Conversely, even a rich, smoky blend like Johnnie Walker Black Label needs fragrant top notes to give it lift and complexity.

Japanese Blends

Japanese blends are also a mix of malt and grain whiskies, but with some subtle differences that define them as Japanese. These stem from wider cultural reasons. These whiskies have always had to respond to the manner in which they have been consumed in Japan, which is different from in the West.

From the outset, this was a drink that was going to be consumed with subtle, delicate Japanese food, a drink that would have to cope with the Japanese climate, especially the humid summers, a drink whose serve would also have to take into account the physiological sensitivity of the Japanese to alcohol.

Everything pointed to lightness. Japan made its blends Japanese: they remain whiskies that are light in nature, but with sufficient weight and character to be able to stand up to Mizuwari levels of dilution (*see* p.34).

Canadian Blends

Scotch blenders will corral a range of whiskies from many different distilleries – often swapping stock – to achieve the desired flavours. Canadian blends, however, are single-distillery whiskies for which all the ingredients are produced under one (often very large) roof. Their root is a high-strength base whisky usually made from corn, but wheat (Highwood) and rye (Alberta) are also used.

To this is then added flavouring whiskies, which are mostly made from a rye base, but corn and barley malt whiskies are also made. By ageing all the whiskies in different types of cask – new and refill American oak and occasionally ex-sherry – the Canadian blenders can further widen the flavour options.

Irish blends

Irish blends are among the fastest-growing whisky brands in the world. In the case of Jameson and Power's (from Irish Distillers) these will be a mixture of a number of grain whiskeys and a selection of single pot still whiskeys. Like their international colleagues, they will age them in a wide selection of different cask types. As a rule of thumb, the older the age statement, the more single pot still whiskey will be included in the blend.

The master blender is an artist who controls the flavours of whisky.

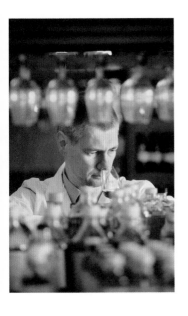

Jameson is no longer a baby, but one of the fastest-growing brands in the world.

Bushmills' blends combine the distillery's own malt and a single grain; the grain and single-malt components for Cooley's Kilbeggan are both produced in-house.

American Blends

American Blended whiskey refers to a blend of grain neutral spirit (not grain whiskey) and straight whiskey.

It would be wrong to think of whisky as slavishly following some fixed formula for centuries. The whisky we drink now is not the same as what was drunk in the 18th, 19th and, in some cases, even the 20th centuries. What was once "empyreumatic" (signed, burned) 200 years ago has become refined.

It has changed because technology, transport, and communication have improved, but most of all because its drinkers have changed.

Flavours are there not just because they are what a distillery makes or a distiller wants – the "Here's my whisky, take it or leave it" approach – but because they have been crafted to show individuality and also give maximum pleasure, all without losing each whisky's soul.

Occasion

Whisky is for every time, but because our palates change depending on how hungry we are or what our mood is, so the drink needs to change to suit the occasion. Having the right whisky for the right occasion is all part of enjoying the spirit. It is also vital in the creation of the whisky. Blenders need to understand occasion – how the whisky is to be enjoyed, by whom, in what climate, in what serve.

Knowing how whisky is made is fascinating for whisky geeks, but is everyone who buys a car given a course on the intricate workings of the internal combustion engine before they make their purchase? Would having that knowledge increase your enjoyment of the drive? In some people's cases, maybe, but most of us buy a car because we can fit the family in it and it will get us from A to B in relative comfort.

It's the same with whisky. We choose it because of familiarity (we like a specific brand), because it suits a serve, but most of all because it fits our mood. By concentrating so hard on the quirks of production we have all forgotten the emotional aspect of whisky – the fact that it is fun, it makes us smile, it is convivial, and its flavours speak to us. This is what is important.

There are moments for each brand. For example, I want something cool, zippy, and stimulating before a meal – a lighter whisky and probably one that will be served long. Relaxing after dinner, however, a bigger and bolder delivery is needed, so I'll search at the richer end of the spectrum. Because I want to maximize the impact of the flavour I'll use less water. The former whisky might be cheaper than the latter, but it is not inferior. It performs brilliantly at the right time and in the right serve. The idea that the more expensive or older the whisky is, the better it will be is not automatically true.

It has always been this way and was something that gained pace during the late 19th century, when whiskies were created to suit cocktails, or to blossom with the splash of soda, in order to become the drink that would be taken before the meal, or the nightcap. Occasion drives everything – choice of brand, style, and serve.

Because of this, understanding the multifarious ways in which whisky can be enjoyed becomes increasingly important – and fun. It is also a completely open field. Saying "This is the best serve" can soon become "This is the only serve", which takes us right back to whisky being a drink that is exclusive, not inclusive.

The modern whisky-drinker is sophisticated, adventurous and resolutely non-traditional.

MIXING

Any time that whisky has achieved popularity has been when it's been diluted. Toddies, Slings, grog, Juleps, the Whisky Punch and the Highball are the drinks that elevated whisky from being a burning, neat spirit drunk for effect into something that people enjoyed consuming. The same applies today. The idea that it should only ever be consumed neat is a new phenomenon.

So, if anyone – friend, bartender, or writer – orders you to drink whisky neat, reach for that bottle of water, my friend, and pour it over their head – saving some for your dram.

ICE

Ice is integral to making a cocktail, while a hand-carved ice ball taken with neat whisky will cool the drink slightly and add just enough dilution to soften the alcohol. That said, I don't like shovelfuls of half-thawed ice (often made with chlorinated water) thrown into a whisky. One or two cubes of hard, pure ice is all that is needed. In a hot climate I'll pass on the water and just have the ice, as the heat will melt the ice and give the right dilution. In a cooler climate I'll pass on the ice and reach for the water. It's about balance.

WATER

This may be the most important thing I'll say in this book: WATER IS YOUR FRIEND.

H_2O not only helps you to (re)hydrate, but is also an essential companion when enjoying whisky. Not only does adding a drop of water when nosing and tasting allow you to appreciate fully the whisky's aromas, but dilution is good when drinking.

It's second nature to me. When growing up, my first "adult" job was the official dilutor of my dad's nightly dram. I learned that the water had to be cold, that its addition would produce strange coiling threads in the liquid and the colour that showed it was just right.

When I was old enough to frequent Glasgow's pubs, there would be small spigots on the bar so that drinkers could dilute drams to their personal preference. If this advanced dispensing method wasn't available, there would always be a water-filled jug.

Why dilution? Because whisky is about pleasure, it is not about pain. Why do many whisky-lovers refuse to add water to 60% ABV whiskies and then grimace as it ignites in their chest, when all of that hurt could so easily be avoided by the addition of some water?

It may seem contradictory for me to say that you should enjoy whisky in whatever way you wish and then tell you one way is wrong, but a drop of water – and sometimes it needs little more than a touch to take the edge off the alcohol – doesn't ruin the whisky, it enhances it. Of the single malts I drink, 90 per cent will be taken this way.

Why Water Works

By reducing the alcohol level, the addition of water kills a whisky's nose burn, making it easier to smell and taste. It also releases flavour. Just as when summer showers allow the hidden aromas of a dry landscape to come alive, so a drop of water energizes whisky.

WHY CARBONATION WORKS

The size and speed of the bubble is important in your fizzy drink. Small bubbles help to deliver more flavour (it is the same with Champagne), but the pressure of the carbonation is also important in creating freshness – and in lessening bitterness on the finish. Fizzy drinks also make you smile.

As Darcy O'Neil writes in his 2010 study of soda fountains, *Fix the Pumps*, when you add CO_2 to water you get carbonic acid. This produces a mildly toxic effect on the tongue, which the body counters by releasing endorphins, which in turn produce a feeling of pleasure. (A heightened sensitivity to this toxic "attack" explains why some people cannot cope with anything fizzy.) In other words if you want to put a smile on the face of the drinker, then add some soda pop.

When the strength of any liquid is above 20% ABV, the ethanol masses like a prison wall around the flavour compounds. When water is added it's like a jailbreak as the ethanol is disturbed and the flavours that are insoluble leap out – straight up your nose.

You can even see this happening through the phenomenon known as viscimetry – the reading of the coils and eddies that appear in the glass when water is added. There are the flavours coming to their fullest expression right in front of your eyes.

MIXERS

We like bubbles. Not only do they make us happy (*see* box, left), but for millennia naturally bubbling mineral water was considered to have health-giving qualities, as the CO_2 allows the mineral salts to be more easily absorbed into the body. By the end of the 18th century, attempts were underway to try to manufacture fizzy water by trapping CO_2 in liquid. By the 1770s, the technique had been solved by Swedish pharmacist Torbern Bergman and in Leeds, England, by the questing mind of Joseph Priestley.

It was Priestley's technique that was improved upon by a man whose name has become synonymous with all things carbonated, Johann-Jacob Schweppe. Schweppe moved from Geneva to London in 1792 to start up commercially. His success wasn't simply because of the novelty of carbonation, but because he had worked out how to bottle his fizzy drink.

Carbonated drinks were taken initially for any number of ailments but, just as spirits had moved quickly from medicinal draught to pleasurable beverage, so Mr Schweppes' Marvellous Waters quickly changed their use from digestive aids to lengtheners and enliveners of spirits – gin with tonic water, and brandy and then whisky with soda or ginger ale.

In 1837, another of our unsung heroes entered the frame with the appearance in Paris of Antoine Perpigna's *vase syphoide*. Perpigna's design for the large dispenser we now know as the soda syphon was developed and improved upon in France and America throughout the 19th century, but the original principles remained the same – a quick and easy delivery of that all-important dash of charged water.

Soda Water (aka Club Soda)
The simplest of the carbonated drinks, this is made by adding bicarbonate of soda to water, which is then carbonated.

Fever-Tree's soda water has the perfect balance for mixing with whisky.

Why it works: The addition of soda water is exactly the same as diluting with still water, only with the added effervescence of carbonation. Carbonation will always add a dry bite which, in soda water, is given a refreshing mineral edge by the addition of the bicarbonate. The dryness of the finish also makes you automatically want to take another sip – not a bad trick!

Fresh, clean, and crisp, soda is like a slightly starchy, morally upright maiden aunt, stern of mien, but with a gentle heart. The minerality at work here when soda water is partnered with smoke adds a light salinity that works beautifully. Conversely, it can make the finish too bitter when paired with some styles. It's not as simple as a splash and a dash.

In the taste test on pages 74–181 I've used Fever Tree Soda Water because of its fantastic balance between crisp delivery, light minerality, and high carbonation, which helps drive the flavour.

Ginger Ale
Brewed, alcoholic ginger beer has been a British speciality from the 18th century onwards and was taken to America 100 years later. It is the lengthener in the classic cocktail, the Mamie Taylor.

Ginger ale, not fermented and lighter in character, started as a Belfast speciality in the 1850s with either Grattan & Co or Cantrell & Cochrane as the originator. This began to be exported to America where a variant called Golden Ginger, with a more pronounced ginger flavour, also started to be made.

Charles Herman Sulz wrote in his 1888 manual, *A Treatise on Beverages*,

> "The great popularity of the Belfast ginger ale is principally due to its fine aroma. All carbonators strive to imitate it as closely as possible, but it is

an unfortunate fact, however, that a great deal of American ginger ale is 'miserable stuff,' in many instances nothing more than sweetened water."

The problem facing many of these early producers was that the ginger lost its intensity quickly. As a result, many began to add capsicum and lemon or lime juice to add bite to their products. It was a Canadian pharmacist, John McLaughlin, who in 1905 created a less sweet Belfast-style version, which he patented two years later as "Canada Dry".

Rye and Ginger was one of the signature drinks of Prohibition-era America, but the mixer's popularity fell away in the face of cola's world domination. Scotch and ginger clung on in the UK until the early 1970s.

Thankfully, these days ginger is on its way back in both beer and ale forms, most often soft, but sometimes "hard" (brewed).

Why it works: For me, the addition of bubbles to ginger-infused water produces whisky's finest mixer, as the ginger is a natural partner with the sweet spices in many whiskies – a by-product of wood ageing – while the drink's energy is enhanced by the bubbles. Importantly, ginger also extends the finish of any whisky.

Ginger is the Rita Hayworth of the mixer world. There's a smouldering, seductive aspect to ginger, which then ignites into spiciness on the kiss-off. In the taste tests on pages 74–181 it came out as the most successful mixer across the board – who couldn't fall in love with Rita? – due to the flavour bridge that it creates between itself and the oak. By having immediate impact on the nose and then a late lift, it's a mixer that enlivens the aroma and lengthens the finish. When it works, it is hard to beat; when it doesn't, it's flat.

The main issue, as Sulz so rightly pointed out back in 1888, is one of balance. Capsicum is often still used instead of ginger, while sugar levels tend to be too high, hiding that essential tingling bite. Remember, ginger ale is a dry mixer.

Again, I have chosen the crisp, clean – and dry – Fever Tree in the taste test, as it uses three types of natural ginger (and no capsicum), which allows the individual whiskies to sing.

Fever-Tree Ginger Ale has the right level of pep and balancing sweetness to give an enhanced whisky drink.

The world's most popular mixer can be a great partner with whisky.

Cola

The roots of the world's biggest-selling soft drink started in France in 1863, when Angelo Mariani created a tonic wine infused with coca leaves.

As Jared Brown and Anistatia Miller reveal in their book *Spiritous Journey* (2009), he also made a spirit-based version whose higher levels of coca made it more... efficacious.

Mariani's idea of using coca as a stimulant in a drink was taken up in 1884 by Atlanta, Georgia-based chemist John S Pemberton, but with the temperance movement already flexing its muscles, he was forced to make his "French Cola Wine" a carbonated soft drink, albeit one that was laced with coca until 1904. It's name? Coca-Cola. Post-Prohibition, colas began their spread to become the world's most popular soft drink, albeit without their original main ingredient.

Why it works: Cola's ubiquity as a soft drink has helped it become the go-to mixer for many spirits, and whisky is no exception. It was cola that elevated blended Scotch to mass-market appeal in Spain in the 1990s, while "Jack 'n' Coke" or "Beam 'n' Coke" have become default calls when an American whiskey is called for.

I've always avoided cola as a mixer and soft drink. There's something about it that's like a slightly wooden B-movie actor. It shouts its presence but has little depth – or so it would seem. While it can easily dominate, bigger whiskies found it to be a sweet partner and, rather than unlocking the secrets of the whisky, in these mixes the whisky seemed to reveal some of the depths of the cola. There's a bridge with vanilla, but those red and black fruits work well with bigger-boned whiskies. There's also something about vermouth that has a passing resemblance to flat cola, and the biggest successes with cola also make great Manhattans and Rob Roys. Maybe that wooden actor was simply given the wrong script.

For me, blended Scotch often struggles to make itself heard above the high levels of sugar in cola, with only the richer or sherry cask-influenced blends faring well. Bourbon's weightier impact works better with it, while the higher levels of vanillin from new oak gives a flavour bridge to the mixer, making it an easier combination. Oh, and don't use "diet" versions! Aspartame and whisky don't rub well up against one another. In these tests I've used Coca-Cola.

Green Tea
Eyebrows tend to raise around the world when this mixer is mentioned. For some, adding green tea simply devalues Scotch, causing it to lose its premium edge, but what cannot be ignored is that Scotch and green tea is a mixing phenomenon, helping the spirit take root in important Asian markets – in particular, China.

Why it works: Bottled (sweetened) green tea is the most common version of this mixer to be used, but the high sugar levels of some brands alter the balance of the drink, making it too saccharine. On the other hand, sugar is important as green tea will have a dry grip that combines with the oak in the whisky, also resulting in an unbalanced drink.

There are two alternatives. Infuse your own green tea, allow it to cool and then mix it with spirit, or choose a bottled brand with low sugar levels. I'd take the former (admittedly time-consuming) option at home using an oolong tea such as Taiwanese Dong Ding, a high-quality white tea, or another lightly oxidized oolong. If using bottled, the trick is to find a medium-dry green tea. Too sweet and the balance is lost, too dry on the other hand and the tannins in the tea form an unholy alliance with those from the oak, giving you a very bitter result. When it works, this is a serious mix with real depth to it. If ginger works horizontally, extending the palate, then green tea goes vertical, adding layers to the mix. It creates a link with whisky's top notes, adding a floral bouquet, forms a natural bridge with the grassy/vegetal notes of some whiskies, and the sweetness gives a point in the middle of the tongue around which all things spin. It's the stern philosopher who suddenly starts dancing.

For the taste test I've used Mr Kon, a low-sugar bottled brand. This gives a gentle, soft undertow without losing the refreshing grassiness of green tea, while adding a very subtle floral lift. Folks, it works!

It might raise eyebrows in the West, but green tea is a popular mixer – and can work well.

Coconut Water

What used to be another eyebrow-raiser, as a drink, is now fast becoming the beverage of choice for health-conscious gym bunnies around the world. Persuading people to mix it with spirits is still a bit of a struggle outside of Brazil – where it is the default mixer with Scotch – but often one sip is all that is needed to make a new convert. As its popularity grows, so its versatility as a mixer will undoubtedly increase.

Why it works: once again the key here is finding a brand with the desired level of sugar. In the taste test, I chose Vita-Coco. I've found it works best with blended Scotch – bourbon and rye clash horribly – although some combinations with light blends end up with a not unpleasant (but not necessarily desired) aroma akin to miso soup. When it works, however, it is superb.

Coconut water is good for you, so there's one reason to drink it. That it can work so well with whisky has been the great revelation of this exercise. Yes it does remind you of Brazil, but there's more to it than just soft, languorous sweetness. Like Tropicalia music – Maria Bethania, perhaps – under the gentleness is some steel, dryness and a little sour note balancing the sweetness. When it works, that almost hidden dry note links with wood to produce a lovely roasted-coconut note, while the sweetness mingles with the soft fruits taking you into luscious fruit-salad territory.

Coconut water is, rightly, becoming one of whisky's most popular companions.

HOW TO DRINK WHISKY

Why have I tasted 102 whiskies in six different ways? I must confess there were times when I was asking myself that very question, but then another surprise would occur and I knew that, while mad, it was a worthwhile undertaking.

There were two underlying reasons. Firstly, because the bulk of whisky enjoyed around the world today is drunk long in some way – maybe with water, maybe softened with ice, often with a mixer, or in a cocktail. Secondly, because no one, to my knowledge, has ever looked at what happens when you pair one whisky with a selection of options and consider which perform best. What was the best way to maximize enjoyment of the bottle, or glass, in front of me? And if there are ideal combinations, could this help people enjoy whisky more, or help more people enjoy whisky?

SCORING SYSTEM

5* The best. A must-try. The whisky transformed into a magnificent drink.

5 Superb. Great enhancement and a seamless mix of the two ingredients, with the whisky revealing more of itself.

4 Great drink. This is where the whisky is beginning to shed some of its seven veils, the drink is more than the sum of its two parts.

3 Good drink, with everything in balance. I'd be happy with one of these. I might not have two.

2 So-so drink with a clash taking place. Seek another option.

1 Avoid.

N/A There are some whiskies for which mixing doesn't work. These are usually great whiskies in their own right.

All of these were tried mixer:whisky in equal parts and at 2:1 and always with ice. Unless otherwise stated, the combination scored was the one at 2:1.

THE LOW-DOWN

The whiskies tasted on pages 74–181 are all widely available, with proven track records. Some great drams had to be excluded – partly because of space, but also because of availability. (Better to know about whiskies you can find than those that remain on the theoretical plane because they are impossible to track down.)

There are more Scotch blends than malts. It is about time that their versatility was discussed. It is also time that malt's air of untouchability was confronted.

I looked for mixes that enhanced the whisky, that took its personality and, by promoting its complexity, offered up new flavours and made it A Great Drink. I make no apologies for speaking of the whiskies as sentient beings; when you see flavours magnified, absorbed – or rejected – in this way, you begin to recognize their personalities.

There were few that performed brilliantly across the board. The vast majority would find one (or more) mixer just a step too far. Some themes emerged: the perfect partnership of smoke and soda water, the reliability of ginger ale, the way in which tannin can be exposed.

It was fascinating to see how some brands, often dismissed by drinkers who insist on only trying them neat, come alive when mixed and suddenly make sense as drinks. Others were real (and pleasant) shocks.

Naturally, there were others who didn't want to play ball. These were the ones with the biggest personalities – sherried malts, straight rye; whiskies with such robust complexities that they were best left on their own. Please don't think, when seeing the scores, that these whiskies are bad in themselves. The scores indicate how good the mix is, not what the quality of the whisky is. If a whisky is best neat, drink it neat. This is a guide to how best to enjoy it.

So work your way through the following pages, try the combinations, enjoy them, and then find your own.

FLAVOUR CAMPS

Each whisky is an individual and yet it is useful to find some commonalities between them – especially to see if there are any generalizations that can be drawn about the best way to drink them. Putting similar whiskies in flavour camps helps with this.

You'll notice that, while the camps for Scotch blends and malts have the same names, I've kept the two styles of whisky apart. This isn't just perversity on my part.

The underlying principle of single malt is to create an individual distillery character – a singularity, if you like. This is then given extra layers of complexity through maturation, but the end result should always have that intense distillery character to the fore.

Blends, on the other hand, are an amalgam of a number of these strong individuals with grain whiskies. They are as complex, but because of the wider spread of these elements the nature of the complexity is different.

A single malt is like a solitary mountain peak. There are supporting flavours, but the peak rises above them. Blends are like a range of rolling hills. They are as beautiful to look at, but are part of a wider landscape. They are not better, or worse. They are different.

SCOTCH, IRISH & JAPANESE BLENDS

These are all blends of single-malt (single pot still in the case of some of the Irish) and grain whisky aged in oak casks.

B1 Light & Fragrant

Here the blender is aiming to produce a light, apéritif whisky – a style created in the 1930s for America, where consumers were asking for lighter characters. Mixability was a significant factor in this. These were the blends that were behind the Second Age of the Highball, which ran up until the late 1960s. Delicate, often floral, they share with malts a "green" character: grapes, melon, pear. The malt component here is skewed towards the estery and intense, the oak is unobtrusive – mainly refill casks are used. Grain is, as always, important here, adding smoothness and sweetness to these prickly and flighty malts, allowing the whole package to float across the tongue. There will, however, be weightier (often sherried) malts hanging around in the background like discreet bodyguards, acting as anchors and giving the whiskies some very subtle structure.

B2 Fruity & Spicy

These blends are medium-weight in character but could possibly contain malts from all four flavour camps. It is the ratio and balance between them that matters. Here you'll find a little more oak at play – in particular from

American oak casks, meaning that there is more vanilla and butterscotch. Lusher, fruitier aromas predominate, rather than being in the supporting role they play in B1, while there are more glimmers of sherry. This greater depth can also be the result of more mature stock being used – a large number here were 12 years or above. This, when combined with the use of first-fill and refill casks, adds more complex, oak-driven weight. Grain adds silkiness and creamy oak, but is downplayed. Because grain is light and often aged in active casks it reaches maturity quickly, allowing it to act like a nanny calming down young, boisterous malts. As the malts mature, they calm down and become more sensible, meaning the grain can take more of a back seat. The equilibrium remains; the manner in which it is achieved has changed.

B3 Rich & Fruity

It is the upping of the sherried element in the mix here that gives these blends their character. These days they're seen as slightly old-fashioned, looking back to a time when the Scotch whisky industry used more sherry casks than American oak. While it is not quite as simple as that – blenders were using refill casks in Edwardian times to produce lighter styles and sherry was still the dominant cask type in the 1930s, when light blends appeared – it's true that the rich, deep blend is less common these days. The blender's skill here is to show the resinous depths of sherry with its sweet, dried-fruit character without allowing the high levels of tannin from the cask to make the blend

too grippy. You don't want your consumers to be picking splinters out of their tongue. Yes, there will be some very active casks used here, but they supply structure rather than flavour. This heavy bass line needs to be ameliorated somehow and once again grain is the key, dissolving tannins, pulling forward fruitiness, allowing some fragrant top notes to rise. Here you are almost reversing the principles of the light and fragrant blends.

B4 Smoky

There has been a noticeable scaling down of smokiness in blends from the 1960s onwards, driven, it is said, by a change in public taste, and yet the largest-selling brand of Scotch – Johnnie Walker – is resolutely smoky. In addition, peaty malts are growing faster than any other style, so who knows? We may see that pendulum swing back once more. The way in which smoke manifests itself in a blend is different to the way in which it performs in a single malt. Because it is just one part of a rich complexity of flavours, the intense almost monomaniacal focus that you get in single malt is reduced, allowing the blanket of smoke to spread across the blend, subtly altering it. The peat is a defining character: adding smokiness, heathery notes, a saline/marine element, but it is nuanced rather than barging in and shoving your nose up a chimney. Once again, grain is important in this process, taking the edge off the smoke, linking it with the other aromas that range, depending on the brand, from the light and fragrant to spicy, fruity, or rich.

SCOTCH, IRISH, JAPANESE & TAIWANESE MALTS

These are whiskies made exclusively from malted barley. Because there was only one single pot still Irish (made from a mix of malted and unmalted barely) tasted, it has been put in this section.

M1 Light & Fragrant

Ahhhh, the smell of springtime: of flowers, cut grass; of fresh fruits like gooseberry, green apple, pear, pineapple. There will also sometimes be a hint of lemon and maybe a flour-sack character. These are light whiskies, delicate to the touch, that show balancing sweetness in the middle of the tongue. Production-wise, these have low wood impact and will be the product of longer fermentation – to help produce these fruity flavours – and a middle cut favouring the flavours that come across early in the process.

M2 Fresh & Fruity

Now, you are beginning to see the influence of the vanilla, coconut, and spice given by first-fill American oak on the distillery character, which itself will have a slightly heavier fruitiness compared to the fragrant camp. Those crisp, green apples have turned into soft orchard fruits like peach, apricot, and, occasionally, mango and guava. Again, long fermentation is used and a slightly wider cut takes place.

M3 Rich & Fruity

Deep, full-bodied, and often slightly more grippy, the influence of ex-sherry casks is what defines these malts. European oak casks have higher levels of tannin and aromas of clove and incense, while the sherry has acted on the oak base to add in walnut, date, raisin, sultana, and treacle. The more first-fill and the longer the time spent in these receptacles, the bigger the whisky will be.

M4 Smoky

The aroma comes from the burning of peat during the kilning process, which takes place at the end of malting. Peat's smoke contains aromatic oils called phenols that stick themselves to the skin of the barley, and this aroma persists all the way through distillation and maturation. The more peat you burn, the more smoky your malt; the later you cut in distillation, the heavier that smokiness will be. Because peat is 3,000-year-old vegetation, its composition varies depending on where it is from. This in turn influences the flavours: heathery from Orkney, smoky and woody from mainland Scotland, and marine and tarry on Islay.

NORTH AMERICAN WHISKIES

From the gentle nature of corn to the feistiness of rye, the whiskes of North America have their own distinct personalities, which results in very different – and exciting – mixing opportunities.

NAM 1 Corn-fed

Here are whiskies where corn is to the fore, adding a deep sweetness and occasionally a "fat" popcorn-like aroma and taste. The straight bourbons in this camp – which could be further sub-divided into light and heavy – have this rich sweetness rather than spicy rye as their dominant character. As these can only be matured in new oak barrels, the influence of the cask will increase the longer the bourbon spends within it – adding further sweetness and depth. Canadian whiskies are blends of different base and flavouring whiskies aged in a variety of different casks. Here a downplaying of the oak element allows the corn to seem sweeter and more pillowy, with notes of maple syrup, butterscotch, and hard candy.

NAM 2 Sweet Wheat

In bourbon, a very different effect is promoted when rye is replaced by wheat in the mashbill. All of the dry spiciness that comes from rye disappears (the only spices therefore coming from the oak) and allowing a more fragrant, floral aspect to be brought forward. They are also more perceptibly sweet. Wheat can also be picked up on the finish, where there is a slight drying.

NAM 3 High Rye

Rye is all about spiciness – think clove, allspice, cumin, cardamom – and also acidity that helps to bring out the tart red fruits in the whiskey. Some can be dry, others dusty, some move into rye-bread territory. What they all have are spices and a physicality. Rye kicks its way in, it crackles, it sours. Straight rye must have a minimum of 51 per cent rye in the mashbill; in the other members of this camp its presence is the dominant one. This applies to bourbon and Tennessee whiskeys as well as Canadian.

SCOTCH BLENDS

While you can make some generalizations about any of these combinations, the fact remains that each brand will put its own spin on what works... and what doesn't.

The lightest blends were, on the whole, happiest with ginger ale – it helped to lengthen their presence. But coconut water was equally strong, bringing out an often hidden sweet core. Fruity blends were where ginger came into its own, with cola especially being too heavy.

The more sherry-accented blends were where soda fell away and cola came to the fore, as its weight and sweetness managed to counteract the grippiness of the whisky. Smoky blends, on the other hand, were at their best with soda – a mix you can do with a great degree of confidence. Ginger was equally happy, but again cola was a no-no.

Green tea showed some variability – it is the most demanding of the partners – but overall was a very sound player right across the spectrum, from light to smoky. Scotch blends, the whisky style created for the Highball, still have some tricks up their sleeve.

100 PIPERS

A big seller in Asian markets, here's a blend that starts sweet and grainy on the neat nose, where fresh sawdust and gooseberry tartness make it slightly edgy. Water brings out a hint of smoke and garam masala spices. A soda mix is fresh and appley, but disconnected. Ginger ale is edgy and slightly too waxy. You're on surer footing with coconut water's nutty/malty combo adding crispness, and while green tea is calmer, allowing canteloupe to come through, it still needs sweetness to soften the finish. The same applies to cola, where its hard kiss-off could be eliminated with some citrus. All very frisky and eager to please, but like a naughty puppy, it needs to be taken in hand.

FLAVOUR CAMP	B1	COLA	3
SODA	2	COCONUT WATER	3
GINGER ALE	2	GREEN TEA	4

ANTIQUARY 12 YEAR OLD

It was The Antiquary's distinctive angled bottle that first caught my eye in a Glasgow jazz pub many years back. It has remained a favourite dram ever since. It remains underappreciated. More should succumb to its steamed syrup pudding of a nose with balanced, popcorn-like grain, while there's just enough light, sweet spice to stop any flabbiness.This chewily luxurious character can be appreciated neat, but I'd go for ginger ale – where the mixer matches the whisky's lushness and extends its length. Cola is a decently dark-fruited match, hinting at how this is one to try in a Rob Roy. Much as I'd love to order an AnTEAquary, it doesn't work.

FLAVOUR CAMP	B2	COLA	4
SODA	3	COCONUT WATER	2
GINGER ALE	4	GREEN TEA	2

BALLANTINE'S FINEST

Imagine you're inside a baker's, your nose assailed by the aromas of pâtisserie, pastries, cakes, and flour, but your sleeve is being tugged by a child who wants you to play in the park on the first day of spring. That's Finest, a mix of the vibrant, grassy, and estery with sufficient sweet softness to give weight – and in blends the more dimensions, the greater the mixability. If you want the energy amplified, go for soda; for a seamless calming drink, head to coconut water; and while green tea is harmonious, watch the tannins. Ginger, however, is perfect. Complex and elegant with the two sweetnesses binding together, freshness and spices offering new accords, it sings.

FLAVOUR CAMP	B1	COLA	2
SODA	4	COCONUT WATER	4
GINGER ALE	5*	GREEN TEA	4

BALLANTINE'S 17 YEAR OLD

Rightly revered as one of the great blends, here we have Ballantine's gentle nature being given extra mature weight. Initially it's all very country house in the autumn: waxed floors, sweet leather, ripe apricots, but a drop of water shows that it has retained some of Finest's apple and freesia freshness. Soda pulls out the extra oak, while cola and coconut both submerge its complexities – evidence that older blends are trickier customers. Ginger remains the mixer to go for, although the waxiness brought out by green tea makes it a fascinating drink. For me, though, I'm happiest with some water or an ice ball – and plenty of time.

FLAVOUR CAMP	B2	COLA	2
SODA	2	COCONUT WATER	2
GINGER ALE	4	GREEN TEA	4

BELL'S

Bell's suffers from overfamiliarity. Wrongly seen as an old person's drink, this old Perth blend deserves a reappraisal. In recent years its spicy, nutty core has been given a fresh, crisp, apple edge, but it's the palate that surprises, as thick and sweet as marmalade. There's plenty going on (and little smoke). Water works, but adding bubbles gives a more satisfying drink, where the soda's dryness contrasts with the sweet palate, pulling out those green fruits. Ginger magnifies the sweet nutty/spicy core and allows it to soar. Cola makes it too nutty; coconut water is bland, and there's a tannin clash with green tea. The old stager mixers are the best here.

FLAVOUR CAMP	B2	COLA	2
SODA	3	COCONUT WATER	3
GINGER ALE	4	GREEN TEA	1

BLACK BOTTLE

For many years, Black Bottle declared itself to have a heart of Islay and as a result became that island's favourite whisky. It was also one of the smokiest blends on the market. Things have changed. A new look and a return to its roots as a rich 19th-century blend has seen the peatiness being dialled back, but extra depth fed in. There's a new mellowness, with black banana, toffee apple, Dundee cake, and hints of cereal with a whiff of spent campfire. Soda allows grassiness to come through, with the rich palate adding weight. Ginger is ripe and full, but a little short. Cola brings out smoke but ends up bitter, while coconut water is bland. Green tea, however, is coolly refreshing with an excellent bold finish. New look, but it remains a versatile player.

FLAVOUR CAMP	B3	COLA	2
SODA	4	COCONUT WATER	2
GINGER ALE	4	GREEN TEA	4

BLACK GROUSE

If The Famous Grouse epitomizes Perth's gentle, calm character, then this, a new member of its growing covey, has a nature that looks to the county's high moors. Though a peaty blend, ginseng, ginger, and peach emerge before the heathery smoke, which itself is balanced by sufficient sherried substance. As smoke and soda are bedfellows that mix is a no-brainer. Cola obliterates everything bar a charred smouldering, but coconut water brings to mind an Ipanema beach bonfire. Green tea moves deliciously into lapsang souchong territory, while ginger is a seamless mix, again accentuating the smoke, but also allowing the sweetness of the mixer and the raisined generosity of the blend to work – a serious drink.

FLAVOUR CAMP	B4	COLA	2
SODA	4	COCONUT WATER	4
GINGER ALE	5	GREEN TEA	4

CHIVAS REGAL 12 YEAR OLD

Originally reformulated in the 1950s to reflect the lighter American palate, Chivas at 12 years might be delicate, but isn't insubstantial. There's a maple-syrup sweetness at work, alongside pineapple and red fruits, while a little dried fruit anchors its dry-grass elements. The fact that it works so successfully with soda is a testament to that fifties reworking. The soda adds immediacy, but none of the sweetness has been lost. Ginger results in a flattening, waxy note, and while cola enhances the rich fruits, it's coconut water that gets the thumbs up, linking with Chivas' nutty aspects and balancing its sweetness. Sadly, though Chivas and green tea is massively popular, it's too dry a combination and you lose the blend's graceful nature.

FLAVOUR CAMP	B1	COLA	3
SODA	4	COCONUT WATER	4
GINGER ALE	3	GREEN TEA	2

CHIVAS REGAL 18 YEAR OLD

Though you might think that Chivas' older expression is just a grown up 12 year old, you'd be wrong. If the younger is a long-limbed teenager, then her older brother has returned from a gap year all mature and glossy. There's a whiff of cigar box alongside the plump peach and honey, while toasted almond and coriander are evidence of his time abroad. Like siblings, what works for one doesn't meet with the other's approval. Soda makes things bitter, coconut water also brings out too much wood, and cola is an overly sweet no-no. Green tea works, showing a floral, fruity element. It's left to ginger to usher in harmony, allowing those scented woods to show themselves.

FLAVOUR CAMP	B2	COLA	2
SODA	2	COCONUT WATER	2
GINGER ALE	4	GREEN TEA	4

CLAN MACGREGOR

Overshadowed by its stablemate Grant's Family Reserve, Clan MacGregor tends to be dismissed as little more than a blend made to hit a price point. Think again. This is a blend made to be mixed (as long as you avoid cola). There's freshness, a light, malty edge, some vegetal notes, and, with water, a lifted, lemony note. Soda steers things too far towards the green zone; there's sweetness needed in the middle, something provided by ginger ale, where the fresh citrus is enhanced. Coconut copes with the vibrancy and is best at high dilution, while the vegetal aspect finds a natural partner with green tea. You see? Not the poor relation at all.

FLAVOUR CAMP	B1	COLA	2
SODA	2	COCONUT WATER	3
GINGER ALE	4	GREEN TEA	4

CUTTY SARK

The blend that started the Jazz Age Charge of the Light Brigade hasn't lost any of its bright-young-thing charms. Cutty is about a porcelain-light coolness: blanched almond, lemon cheesecake, vanilla, balanced by almost hidden silky depths. No surprise that it works brilliantly with soda, an instantly appetizing, moreish, lightly herbal drink where the crispness of the mixer plays off the sweetness, revealing perfumed notes. Ginger is slightly too gingery, and while cola pulls out sherried depths it's to the detriment of balance. Go instead for the fresh, iced-melon flavours of a mix with coconut water or the floral lift of green tea. Cool in every sense.

FLAVOUR CAMP	B1	COLA	2
SODA	5*	COCONUT WATER	4
GINGER ALE	3	GREEN TEA	4

DEWAR'S WHITE LABEL

There's something sweet about all the old Perth blends, and White Label, one of the first great global Scotch brands, is the sweetest of the lot. Think mashed banana and melting white-chocolate ice cream given just the right amount of spicy energy by clove and mace on the finish. Nothing surprises it – the nuttiness given by green tea is akin to Japanese Hoji-cha, and though coconut water is a little obtrusive, a 1:1 makes a gentle, soft mix. Cola emphasizes the spices and a scented, floral element. The dryness of soda doesn't obscure the sweet spot, instead adding complexity, but this is another where ginger wins out – the two sweet elements and the spicy tail all work in harmony.

FLAVOUR CAMP	B1	COLA	4
SODA	4	COCONUT WATER	3
GINGER ALE	5	GREEN TEA	3

DEWAR'S 12 YEAR OLD

Sometimes there's a mixer that steps up and takes a whisky into another dimension. Often you can second-guess what it's going to be, but Dewar's 12 year old and green tea come out of left field. You might expect that other mixers would work better with this richer, layered take on the sweet Dewar's template. It comes over like a hedonistic Caribbean holiday, all cocoa butter suntan lotion, anise, honey, and mango. It works, at 2:1, with soda; coconut water is a bit of a no-brainer; cocoa comes out with cola, while ginger spins the tropical aspects into candied peels. But green tea elevates this to a classic drink: complex, floral, rich, sweet, and sumptuous.

FLAVOUR CAMP	B2	COLA	3
SODA	3	COCONUT WATER	3
GINGER ALE	4	GREEN TEA	5*

FAMOUS GROUSE

Here's another Perth blend where easy-going is the defining character. Everything is just so well-balanced: orange peel for zestiness, banana for lift, green olive for vibrancy, toffee grain to smooth, nutty/raisin sherry element for depth. All there, but understated. Soda is a little firm, though an upping of the grassy element makes it exciting. Green tea is pleasant but both elements are separate rather than linked, and cola rides roughshod over the mix. Better is ginger ale that fleshes out the mid-palate and extends the finish – try this as a Mamie Taylor. Coconut water adds a sweet weight and a light, dry finish, offering the best partner of all the mixes for this well-balanced blend.

FLAVOUR CAMP	B2	COLA	2
SODA	3	COCONUT WATER	4
GINGER ALE	4	GREEN TEA	3

GRANT'S FAMILY RESERVE

Quietly, unshowily, Grant's Family Reserve has risen to become the world's third-largest-selling blended Scotch. What has the world fallen in love with? Freshness, certainly, but backed with silky grain, toasted marshmallows, almond flakes, cut flowers, a little waxiness, and dark chocolate. Soda is fine: there's added mashed fruit, but the minerality is a little harsh. Green tea swamps it, but a harmony is reached with coconut water, thanks to the soft grain, while sufficient oak adds texture. Ginger is restrained until a drop of orange bitters sparks things into life, but it's cola, which often struggles with Scotch, that surprises here, playing a supporting role, allowing light smoke and a gentle fruitiness to develop.

FLAVOUR CAMP	B2	COLA	5
SODA	3	COCONUT WATER	3
GINGER ALE	4	GREEN TEA	2

GRANT'S 12 YEAR OLD

There's often a step-change with blends at 12 years of age, when the freshness of youth is replaced by depth and maturity – the grains have weight, the malts become fully expressive. This is demonstrated perfectly here: a mix of chocolate and flowers with crisp cereal working quietly in the background. The grain adds a rummy note, while the palate is all tweed, dusty spices, and light lavender. It's happy with its own company; keep it away from green tea and coconut water. Cola, here does little, but the two old-timers show personality: ginger giving increased sweetness, while soda adds extra lift, not in an overexcited fashion, just a gentle raising of a well-mannered eyebrow. Maturity, you see.

FLAVOUR CAMP	B2	COLA	3
SODA	5	COCONUT WATER	1
GINGER ALE	4	GREEN TEA	2

GREAT KING STREET

After shaking up the world of malts by vatting them, John Glaser of Compass Box decided to do the same for blends by, er, blending, but doing so with a high malt:grain ratio and upping the first-fill oak element. Result? American cream soda, pears, lily of the valley and a luscious palate tickled by green cardamom and anise before white peaches appear. This blossoms into life with soda, becoming a complex mixed drink with length and class. Ginger ale is equally strong, with the spice giving the slow-release palate a boost. Coconut water ends up spirity and cola has too much charred wood, but green tea offers masses of soft, tropical fruits, jasmine leafiness, and weight. World class.

FLAVOUR CAMP	B2	COLA	2
SODA	5*	COCONUT WATER	3
GINGER ALE	4	GREEN TEA	4

HANKEY BANNISTER

Here's a classic example of how tasting a blend neat only gives you a partial picture of its true personality. When Mr Hankey's quaking and naked you get nuttiness, clotted cream, and fruit cake. Though it opens slightly with water, it's best to dive in with soda, which has a transformative effect, shedding the nutshell and allowing estery grassiness to link with the toffee core. Ginger ale latches on to the citrus and is a sound mix, and though green tea is pretty simple, when mixed with cola there's a lovely cherry note and a reduction in sweetness. The blend allows coconut water to take charge, but adds a pleasant nuttiness to the finish. You see? Mixing is essential.

FLAVOUR CAMP	B1	COLA	4
SODA	3	COCONUT WATER	4
GINGER ALE	3	GREEN TEA	3

J&B

One glance at J&B and you can see how everything is pushed as far as it can be towards the light: pale in hue, lightly dusty, with pear drops, lime blossom, unripe pears, and (dilute) the fragrance of a clean rabbit hutch. Matching it with soda adds a slight salinity, while ginger ale has scented qualities and that lime note, but it's fleeting – this is a blend for people with a five-second attention span. It bends like a palm in a storm to accommodate coconut water and green tea, giving pleasant drinks but not identifiably J&B drinks. Weirdly, it's best with cola, where maltiness is offset by sweetness, which in turn is cut through by the inherent freshness.

FLAVOUR CAMP	B1	COLA	4
SODA	3	COCONUT WATER	3
GINGER ALE	3	GREEN TEA	3

JOHNNIE WALKER RED LABEL

Maybe it's the confidence in being the the world's biggest-selling blend, but Johnnie Walker Red isn't exactly shy, enthusiastically leaping out of the glass with gingery spice, lemon rind, red fruit, and heathery smoke. The grain acts like a sprung dance-floor, allowing the boisterous elements to bounce on top. Mixing with soda sees it at its most refreshing: the smoke and minerality do their double act after a sweet, soft palate. Ginger is a no-brainer, with classic vibrancy and the smoke running subtly beneath. Cola picks out sweetness, though the burned edges given by the peat might be too much for some, while coconut water, also sweet, cuts down the smoke, but adds in banana. Green tea is more successful, flashing between citrus, grass, and light smoke.

FLAVOUR CAMP	B4	COLA	3
SODA	5	COCONUT WATER	2
GINGER ALE	5*	GREEN TEA	4

JOHNNIE WALKER BLACK LABEL

Walker Black is a resonant mix of autumn orchards and seashore – black fruits, fruit cake, and fragrant smoke. Like a well-mannered gentleman it is at ease in all company, solicitously giving enough of itself to boost its partner's confidence. The smoke-and-soda combo works its magic, with an added sweet depth. Ginger is a sophisticated partnering, with sweetness and fragrance and a complex length. It tolerates cola, offering up dark elements, and though green tea is less compelling, it's pleasant. With coconut water it puts on a white suit and relaxes as its partner mingles and teases out new flavours, including a gentle roasted element. Nothing seems to faze its debonair charms.

FLAVOUR CAMP	B4	COLA	3
SODA	5	COCONUT WATER	5
GINGER ALE	5*	GREEN TEA	3

JOHNNIE WALKER GOLD LABEL RESERVE

Launched to replace the previous 18-year-old Gold Label, this new arrival to the Walker stable retains its predecessor's succulence. You're in a farmhouse kitchen with honeycomb, tangerine marmalade, and fresh buttered scones on the table. A fresh sea breeze carries light smoke, which, as we know, will be sniffed out by soda, though the ratio needs to be 1:1 to retain that soft centre. Cola is a car crash, while green tea makes it weirdly leathery, and though coconut water works, once again it's Walker and ginger that is the most effective. The smoke drifts, the layers of honey and cashew are amplified, the length is extended, but again, drop it to 1:1. Or have it on the rocks.

FLAVOUR CAMP	B2	COLA	1
SODA	4	COCONUT WATER	3
GINGER ALE	4	GREEN TEA	2

OLD PARR 12 YEAR OLD

Like many venerable blends, Old Parr's character harks back to when the richness and weight given by sherry casks were the norm. The trick with this type of blend is to balance the leather Chesterfield comfort of raisin, date, and walnut with lightness and fragrance – here in the guise of flamed orange peel, caraway, and coriander. Water brings out a thick, fruity, blackcurrant chewiness, meaning that sweeter mixers work best – soda is too dry, ginger no more than fair. Coconut shows solidity, length, and creaminess, while green tea makes a bold combination, with allspice and flowers, but pales compared to cola, which produces a classy mixed drink: plummy and deep. Old Parr also works excellently as the base for a Rob Roy.

FLAVOUR CAMP	B3	COLA	5
SODA	2	COCONUT WATER	4
GINGER ALE	3	GREEN TEA	4

ROYAL SALUTE 21 YEAR OLD

Whatever the latest term is to describe top-end Scotch (ultra-super-premium?), Royal Salute has pedigree as an elegant blend of great complexity and depth, *i.e.* it's one of the blends that malt purists need to try. The nose opens like a sandalwood chest of dried tropical fruits, and this exotic musk/leather note continues to unfold alongside signature Chivas sweetness, while necessary lift comes in the form of redcurrant. This is a plush and sumptuous a blend as you'll find. I tried it with the mixers in different ratios, but none enhanced a dram already at maximum expressiveness. Younger blends need mixing, some older ones are best just left on their own.

FLAVOUR CAMP	B3	COLA	N/A
SODA	N/A	COCONUT WATER	N/A
GINGER ALE	N/A	GREEN TEA	N/A

SCOTTISH LEADER

A dram not exactly shy at coming forward. A very punchy nose drives forward cream toffee and a pleasant note of gammon steak. There's something of a greengrocer's shop about it, and it's this fruitiness that dominates the palate with a physical thickness in the middle of the tongue. All very straightforward. Soda is too salty, and while there's dried fruit with ginger it's no better than a good mix. Green tea picks out the sweet core and allows the layers to develop, while coconut water shows roasted coconut at its most substantial. Cola has red and black fruits playing off each other: ripe, rich, and weighty. Not straightforward at all.

FLAVOUR CAMP	B3	COLA	5
SODA	2	COCONUT WATER	4
GINGER ALE	3	GREEN TEA	4

TEACHER'S

One of the last of the old Glasgow blends, Teacher's has retained the smoky weight that singled out the city's drams. Deep and complex with ripe fruits, malt loaf, and boot polish, it's given needed lift by jags of lemon and menthol. It struggles with green tea – too much earthy smoke – and while cola gives an intriguing liquorice note, it's pretty OTT. It's the smoke that's enhanced by ginger's crisp, dry edge, but orange is needed. There's no prevarication with coconut water: a marriage of smoke, rooty elements, sweetness and thick texture. Ultimately, though, it's soda that makes it fly and show its real complexity – and makes a proper, grown-up whisky drink.

FLAVOUR CAMP	B4	COLA	3
SODA	5	COCONUT WATER	4
GINGER ALE	3	GREEN TEA	2

WHITE HORSE

White Horse remains one of the few resolutely smoky blends. That dry peatiness is given a counterpoint on the palate by soft, generous grain before an energetic, fresh (and smoky) finish. When you add mixers, though, this horse gallops. One sip with soda and you can see why it was called "charged water" – this has an electric effect, the complexities of the palate are revealed and the mineral/salt, smoke, and sweetness of the finish leave you gasping for more. Ginger has a pleasing bittersweet edginess, and though cola and green tea are passable, coconut water comes over like another Brazilian beach barbecue, while the whisky does a Scottish samba on the tongue.

FLAVOUR CAMP	B4	COLA	1
SODA	5	COCONUT WATER	4
GINGER ALE	3	GREEN TEA	1

WHYTE & MACKAY

Undoubtedly, "big-boned" is an insult in some situations, but not, I feel, in whisky. Whyte & Mackay is one such amply proportioned blend, where treacle, coffee, and strawberry jam mix with a subtle smokiness and rich dried fruits. The use of sherried cask is lavish, but there's enough lift to give it balance. The sherried weight causes issues with mixing, though: soda is too crisp, while ginger struggles, and coconut water turns into miso soup. Help is at hand with green tea that turns almost Darjeeling-like but has perfumed floral layers. Cola meets it head-on and in a mighty tussle promotes all those deep, burned dark fruits. Not shy, not delicate. Big-boned.

FLAVOUR CAMP	B3	COLA	4
SODA	1	COCONUT WATER	2
GINGER ALE	2	GREEN TEA	3

WILLIAM LAWSON'S

Once seen as the makeweight in a Bacardi stable, which contains big-hitter Dewar's, William Lawson's is one of the fastest-growing blends in the world, thanks mainly to Russia. Clearly there's something about this fruity little number with its flashes of white pepper, toffee apple, and sweet spice, though it's pretty hidden with soda water, which does its occasional "pick up the fresh elements and make them really unripe" trick. Cola and green tea are honest enough, but coconut water shows a gentle loveliness, bringing out hidden ripe fruits without losing the energy – which, along with sweet spices, is the key to the most successful fusion: with ginger ale. Oh, those Russians.

FLAVOUR CAMP	B1	COLA	3
SODA	2	COCONUT WATER	4
GINGER ALE	4	GREEN TEA	3

WINDSOR 12 YEAR OLD

Once a Korean exclusive, the well-bred Windsor family is now beginning to travel across Asia. Its 12 year old is a hugely gentle, sweet, and creamy blend, like eating vanilla and apricot ice cream with a syrup and hazelnut topping. There's a certain delicacy, meaning soda is best in equal amounts to show fully a caramel and marzipan character. Ginger also needs to be lightly handled to give a zesty finish. Cola brings out ripe papaya and a light charred note, while fruits appear with coconut water (apples) and green tea (pear, guava). A splash of water or rock of ice is equally good. How very well behaved.

FLAVOUR CAMP	B2	COLA	3
SODA	4	COCONUT WATER	4
GINGER ALE	3	GREEN TEA	3

SCOTCH MALTS

The assumption is that malts don't mix, or from a more fundamentalist point of view, shouldn't be mixed. While this is undoubtedly true for some, the average scores replicated those of Scotch blends pretty much across the board.

What you are dealing with here is greater levels of intensity, meaning there was greater variability within each camp. One combination might work, but the next one would do the opposite. Whereas blends seem to want to please, malts tend to be more unpredictable.

In general terms, however, for the lightest, choose soda, ginger ale, and coconut water, but avoid cola or green tea. The fruity camp saw the old classics having clear bubbles between them, and the rest saw coconut water outperforming cola.

Sherried malts weren't as comfortable with cola as malts had been, those higher tannin levels also made them problematic with coconut water and, predictably, green tea.

Smoke again flew with soda – the highest average score of any combination – showing that mixing with malts can be worthwhile, but the rest were more patchy.

Looking deeper into the combinations it was apparent that while a simple mix didn't always produce a spectacular result, there was enough to suggest that a twist of citrus would be sufficient to make it so. Equally, ginger, coconut water or green tea could be used as a component within a cocktail. Malts: mixable, but always on their own terms.

ABERFELDY 12 YEAR OLD

Well lay me down and smear me in honey! That's the thought that springs to mind when encountering Aberfeldy neat, with a rock, or a splash of water for the first time. Here we have one of the most hedonistic single malts: thick honeycomb and Greek yoghurt with blobs of strawberry jam and fresh peach. Seduced yet? Try it with an equal amount of soda to discover its floral aspects, or ginger to see more of the sweet oak. The others are less successful – most surprisingly coconut water, where the mix veers rapidly into (too) dry territory. Green tea has fragrance but little else, cola is tricky. They're not bad, but what's the point of Aberfeldy if it's not sexy?

FLAVOUR CAMP	M2	COLA	2
SODA	4	COCONUT WATER	2
GINGER ALE	3	GREEN TEA	3

ABERLOUR A'BUNADH

The Aberlour range is vast (and sightly baffling), with flavours that move from cereal, to toffee, to fruity, or vanilla-led – always, though, with a little lift of blackcurrant. With cask-strength A'bunadh it's at its biggest, boldest, and least compromising. A mahogany colour with hints of ruby means only one thing: first-fill sherry casks. No surprise that this cult malt is a compressed mass of hawthorn, prunes, and, yes, currant bound together with resin. There's a little meaty sulphur with water, but the palate for such a strong beast is remarkably gentle. Take it slow, take it with a little water, but take my advice and don't try to mix with it.

FLAVOUR CAMP	M3	COLA	N/A
SODA	N/A	COCONUT WATER	N/A
GINGER ALE	N/A	GREEN TEA	N/A

ARDBEG 10 YEAR OLD

There's a cockiness about Ardbeg at 10 years. There's no smooth talk, no subtle circumvention. It eyeballs you, says, "You want smoke? I got it." As a result, it's easy to overlook what's happening behind. That smoke is a mix of the seashore and the sooty confines of a smokehouse, but there's also lime, moss, apple, and bay leaf. Soda is like a crony urging his gang leader on, adding salinity and drive. Ginger supplies a strange artichoke note; cola disappears under increased smoke, while green tea can't find a way to get involved. The only time it is subdued is when it is gently stretched out on the beach, calmed by by the murmurings of coconut water.

FLAVOUR CAMP	M4	COLA	3
SODA	4	COCONUT WATER	4
GINGER ALE	3	GREEN TEA	2

ARRAN MALT 14 YEAR OLD

The days of writing about The Arran as Scotland's newest distillery are long gone. Now at a positively middle-aged 14 years, it has developed a pleasant rounded belly to go with its biscuity core and spicy, flamed-orange-peel and barley-sugar top notes. Soda's mineral content adds a little too much bitterness to the mix, while the whisky's maltiness rises too high with coconut water. Cola, though slightly woody, makes a decent drink, but it's green tea and ginger that work best. The former gives aromatic lift, and though a little sweetness is needed, there is the basis of a good mix here. The latter comes in all guns blazing: balanced, vibrant, and the perfect companion.

FLAVOUR CAMP	M2	COLA	3
SODA	2	COCONUT WATER	2
GINGER ALE	4	GREEN TEA	3

BALVENIE DOUBLEWOOD

This is a seemingly unflappable malt. No matter which type of cask you put Balvenie in, it will gently, elegantly work in harmony. Here, the runny flower honey and light cereal of the distillery are given licks of vanilla and dried fruits from oak, emerging with extra stewed fruit. Soda makes an appropriately serious and lightly scented drink at 1:1, and while cola has a slightly odd intensity, there's enough in the cherry, vanilla, and herbal aromas to suggest a Rob Roy would work. Then, good-natured Balvenie turns. Ginger is flat; with coconut it gets in a huff and refuses to mix, while with green tea it's a teenager saying, "Talk to the hand." Everything has its limits, even Balvenie.

FLAVOUR CAMP	M3	COLA	3
SODA	4	COCONUT WATER	2
GINGER ALE	2	GREEN TEA	1

BOWMORE 12 YEAR OLD

Those who haven't visited Islay tend to think of it as a small, wet island, and while horizontal rain is known, on sunny days, with opalescent seas and white sand beaches, you could be in the Caribbean. Almost. That's what is captured in Bowmore. Yes, there's Islay's fragrant peat-smoke and a smack of brine, but there's also white peach and mango behind. This tropicality is revered by malt-lovers and is brought out by simple mixes. Soda has it, alongside discreet smoke; ginger takes that and adds sweet spices; the fruit salad offers softness to cola, and though green tea is grippy, coconut water is, obviously really, a no-brainer: guava, papaya, mango, light smoke, length. The sun is shining.

FLAVOUR CAMP	M4	COLA	4
SODA	5	COCONUT WATER	5
GINGER ALE	4	GREEN TEA	3

BRUICHLADDICH
10 YEAR OLD

It's as impossible to dislike Bruichladdich as it is to hate a sad-eyed puppy. You cannot be offended by such a soft and fresh malt with aromas of lemon, daffodils, cream, hot sand, and a sweet centre like chocolate malted milk. All roll along the tongue until perky spices finish things off. It's a little too soft for cola to work, while green tea does its "I don't like wood" thing. With a twist of orange, ginger fuses with the finish; otherwise it would be just too dry. Soda, meanwhile, reveals a little of the malty heart. Coconut, with its sweet/sour element, is a good mix, with added charred elements.

FLAVOUR CAMP	M2	COLA	1
SODA	3	COCONUT WATER	3
GINGER ALE	4	GREEN TEA	2

CARDHU 12 YEAR OLD

There's a prevailing misapprehension with single malt that equates light with bland, which is a bit like saying that Manny Pacquiao would have been better off as an accountant. Cardhu is a bantamweight with a similarly focused intensity. Citric, grassy, spicy, it bounces across the palate and has the acidic finish that is so useful when it comes to mixing. It is light though, so be careful with dilution – I'd go for rocks rather than water. Use equal parts of soda for a fresh, orange-zest lift. The same for a perfect – and happily long – marriage with ginger. Cola, while more of a struggle, has a certain brio, but green tea fails and coconut is no more than average.

FLAVOUR CAMP	M2	COLA	3
SODA	4	COCONUT WATER	2
GINGER ALE	4	GREEN TEA	2

GLENFARCLAS 15 YEAR OLD

One of the old-school Speyside malts, Glenfarclas is best known for its adherence to direct-fired stills and sherry wood; and while this 15 year old is light in hue, it's the rich, almost burned note from the distillation and dried-fruit (sultana) punch that dominate, but not so much that agave syrup, strawberry, and rose water aren't seen. A big package of flavours, it sits uneasily with cola and coconut water (soupy elements in both), and soda is little more than just bubbly water. Ginger, though, is lovely, with the sweetness coming forward as dried fruits chase behind. Unusually for sherried whiskies, green tea shows great balance. Non-traditional, but it works.

FLAVOUR CAMP	M3	COLA	1
SODA	2	COCONUT WATER	1
GINGER ALE	4	GREEN TEA	4

GLENFIDDICH 12 YEAR OLD

The world's biggest-selling malt has been putting on a little weight recently. Don't fear; it's still sweet, with lots of pear and banana and orchard fruits, but alongside the vanilla is some sweet dried fruit and an extra chewiness to the palate. Soda (at 1:1) pushes the fresh, green, spring-like elements to the fore, along with anise and lavender – a slice of apple might just do the trick here. Ginger takes the crunch of apple and mushes it nicely into the soft fruits. Green tea is too dusty and there's a strange wet-leather note that rises off cola. Coconut could work with a little tweaking. In other words, there's lots of potential here.

FLAVOUR CAMP	M1	COLA	1
SODA	4	COCONUT WATER	3
GINGER ALE	3	GREEN TEA	2

GLENFIDDICH 15 YEAR OLD

Plum jam on warm, buttered wholemeal toast. That's what rises to meet you out of a glass of this *solera*-vat-married malt. Here is Glenfiddich at its most avuncular, an all-embracing, warming mix of blue fruits and chocolate, gentle, yet substantial. The herbaceous intensity given by soda is therefore a surprise, but not at high dilution. Ginger is balanced but nothing ignites, and while there's a touch of sloe with cola, the whisky drowns in its depths. Coconut water produces Bounty bars on the nose, but has a hard landing, while with green tea the tannin clash happens. There's sufficient complexity to make great cocktails – or just enjoy on its own.

FLAVOUR CAMP	M3	COLA	3
SODA	3	COCONUT WATER	2
GINGER ALE	2	GREEN TEA	2

GLEN GRANT 10 YEAR OLD

Major Grant, the Edwardian owner of this distillery, had greenhouses in its grounds where he grew fantastical fruits the likes of which the natives of Rothes had never seen. There's still something of the hothouse about his whisky's nose: banana, melon skin, and kiwi, lychee and flowers. It's all very clean, fragrant, and crisp with a lightly creamy palate. You need to be careful with dilution. Soda at 1:1 is a cool drink – try adding cucumber or mint. Ginger and cola are both too dominant, the latter producing a dustiness. The more exotic (for Scotland) mixes, however, work nicely. Coconut water needs to be cold and long, while green tea is aromatic, clean, and balanced. Those greenhouses are still at work.

FLAVOUR CAMP	M1	COLA	2
SODA	4	COCONUT WATER	3
GINGER ALE	2	GREEN TEA	3

THE GLENLIVET 12 YEAR OLD

Breakfast in bed on Mother's Day. Could anything be more delightful? Here we have a big bunch of cut flowers, cream, nectarine juice, fruit salad (apple and pineapple), and then white pepper (a child has been involved in the making of the feast). The last thing you want therefore is for this loveliness to be shattered, so steer clear of both coconut water and green tea. Cola seems slightly strange, but a herbal/rooty note does develop. Better is soda – lots of crisp fruits and dry minerality, a thirst-quencher when short. Ginger is vibrant and energetic with the breakfast tray given a new summeriness by heather blossom. A happy day in store.

FLAVOUR CAMP	M1	COLA	3
SODA	3	COCONUT WATER	2
GINGER ALE	4	GREEN TEA	2

THE GLENLIVET 18 YEAR OLD

The freshness of the 12 year old has here been replaced by something deeper. Those green apples have turned red, the pineapple is now roasted, the flowers have dried slightly, the breakfast tray is now a cedar cigar box. There are touches of sherry, toffee, and rhubarb. It all makes you wonder how good it will be mixed. It doesn't start well with green tea (a collapse), while coconut water splits, and cola is an unnecessary effort. Soda, (at 2:1) however, makes an excellent, firm, lemony drink with the oak calmed down, and ginger is the best fusion with energy, life, and complexity.

FLAVOUR CAMP	M3	COLA	3
SODA	4	COCONUT WATER	2
GINGER ALE	4	GREEN TEA	1

GLENMORANGIE THE ORIGINAL

Hedonism isn't a quality people associate with us Scots. Naturally I disagree, but Glenmorangie The Original disproves it considerably more successfully. This is a sensual, sybaritic melange of orange, guava, and passion fruit, topped with hazelnuts and mint, then enfolded in clotted cream. You'd think that soda would be too dry; instead night-scented stocks are added – but have it short. Ginger is subtle and harmonious, the spices adding length and introducing saffron and a peppery note with higher dilution. Cola isn't hedonistic so leave well alone, and coconut isn't as easy as you'd think, adding some florals but the added sourness is a barrier. Green tea, however, is estery and floral. Point proved, methinks.

FLAVOUR CAMP	M2	COLA	2
SODA	5	COCONUT WATER	3
GINGER ALE	5	GREEN TEA	3

HIGHLAND PARK 12 YEAR OLD

To Orkney and a malt that seems to be in every Scottish distiller's list of top drams. Yes, there is smoke but it's not at heavy Islay levels. Instead it sits behind the chewy toffee, bitter orange peel, black banana, and toffee fudge adding little fragrant, heathery notes. This is made more obvious with water: adding sandalwood and old cigar smoke. It is strangely difficult to mix with, though. Soda is crisp but there's enough sweetness on the palate to balance; ginger, in the way of some malts, seems flat; cola is a waste of everyone's time; coconut water is a tough one; and by now you know all about green tea when it doesn't work. Here, the simplest serve works best.

FLAVOUR CAMP	M4	COLA	1
SODA	3	COCONUT WATER	2
GINGER ALE	2	GREEN TEA	1

HIGHLAND PARK
18 YEAR OLD

There's an Orcadian chair design in which the sitter is cocooned from the draught by a giant wicker hood, an image that springs to mind with this interior dram: peats on the fire, plates of gingerbread and toffee, jars of marmalade and candied peels. Warming and rich, there are a lot of sherried notes that make mixing a worry. Soda retains richness and the smoke, but it almost overbalances; with ginger there's added juniper and liquorice root, suggesting it could be an element in a more complex drink. Cola again is a no-no, as is coconut, and green tea is a battle that needs to be brought to a swift conclusion. Have it by the fire on its own.

FLAVOUR CAMP	M3/4	COLA	1
SODA	3	COCONUT WATER	1
GINGER ALE	3	GREEN TEA	1

KILCHOMAN MACHIR BAY

Although it only started in 2005, Kilchoman doesn't have any of the rubbery explosion-in-a-prophylactic-factory notes of many young, smoky malts. Instead the peatiness is balanced by fleshy fruits, allowing smouldering fires to mix with mint, pear, and clove. There's plenty of oyster brine and beach bonfire notes with soda, but the oiliness means it doesn't become too dry – a Killa-Hiball. Ginger has spice, smoke, and some creamy fruits. Cola is like your clothes the morning after a bonfire. A lovely match is made with coconut water, where smoky pineapple greets you, and green tea is like a cup of lapsang souchong in a Shanghai antiques store. Quite something for one so young.

FLAVOUR CAMP	M4	COLA	3
SODA	5*	COCONUT WATER	5
GINGER ALE	3	GREEN TEA	4

KNOCKANDO 12 YEAR OLD

A wispy, fragile, ethereal thing Knockando is. Clean and slightly nutty, there's a flour-mill dustiness to it, even some of the cooked bran in the background, but a fluffy lemon sweetness stops it from becoming too dry. No fear of oak getting in the way here; the issue is dryness, but soda brings out a real sweetness, and ginger also works extremely well at sweeping that dusty element away, because it is helping to add more sweetness and length. Cola, coconut water, and green tea all work well because of the lack of wood. In fact, to get the most out of this dram, go long!

FLAVOUR CAMP	M1	COLA	3
SODA	4	COCONUT WATER	3
GINGER ALE	4	GREEN TEA	3

LAGAVULIN 16 YEAR OLD

Lagavulin takes you into a parallel Islay. The signature shoreline notes are there, there's laurel and thyme, but also a heightened Tibetan-like exoticism of burning juniper, incense, and lapsang souchong. It frowns at you when you suggest mixing, but soda allows smoke and seaweed to come through; while ginger is like smoking rough shag on a fishing boat. There's an initial mutual respect with coconut water, but Lagavulin soon stomps off; and though you'd think there might be a connection with green tea, there's just too much in the whisky. The most astonishing revelation is how it goes so well with equal parts of cola. Huge, bitter, with smoked meats: rich and sweet. If purists hate the idea, make 'em a Rob Roy.

FLAVOUR CAMP	M4	COLA	5
SODA	4	COCONUT WATER	2
GINGER ALE	4	GREEN TEA	2

LAPHROAIG 10 YEAR OLD

There's a different smokiness at work here, one that drags you to railroad sleepers by the seashore. It's drier, earthy, and creosote-like, with some iodine, but there's custardy softness and sweet roasted malt sitting patiently in the background. They're the key in mixing. Smoke and soda are partners like Butch Cassidy and the Sundance Kid, and here there are added fir and wintergreen notes and a soft centre. Ginger makes things overtly medicinal but sweet, with smoke coming through at the back. With cola, if anything the smoke is upped, and though coconut water initially seems more linear, the mix is anchored by that malty sweetness allowing the smoke to drift free. It works a treat – unlike, sadly, green tea.

FLAVOUR CAMP	M4	COLA	4
SODA	5	COCONUT WATER	4
GINGER ALE	3	GREEN TEA	2

MACALLAN GOLD

Sherried whiskies come in many forms; not all are necessarily big and tannic. This Macallan shows a lighter side, one with a warm, prickling, yeasty element, some light almond, and slightly singed brioche with sultana, hay, and dried apricots. Soda at 1:1 manages to tame all of this down successfully, allowing the real sweetness of the whisky to come through, along with some finesse – better than with water. Ginger and sherry can struggle and that's the case here, and while a cola mix's nose brings out the oxidized notes, there's a clash on the palate. Coconut lacks harmony and unsurprisingly tannins clash with with green tea. The key? Keep it simple with soda or ice – and keep it strong.

FLAVOUR CAMP	M2	COLA	2
SODA	4	COCONUT WATER	2
GINGER ALE	1	GREEN TEA	1

MACALLAN 18 YEAR OLD (SHERRY)

Rightly regarded as the definitive expression of Macallan, the 18 years spent in ex-sherry casks has added dark, resinous notes of plum, date, walnut, shoe wax, raisin, and iron-tinged molasses to the meaty Macallan core of cereal and oil. Because it is such a heavy spirit the tannins aren't troublesome when tasted neat or with a little water – where more fruits come through. The same can't be said when you try to mix with it. Soda is the simplest of them all, but the wood clashes with the dry starchiness of the mixer. The same goes in varying degrees with the others. Here is one that is quite definitely best left naked.

FLAVOUR CAMP	M3	COLA	N/A
SODA	N/A	COCONUT WATER	N/A
GINGER ALE	N/A	GREEN TEA	N/A

MONKEY SHOULDER

This "blended malt" was created to try and tempt bourbon drinkers into Scotch, though to this nose it tips its hat towards Canada rather than Kentucky. Clean and sweet, there's a lot of American oak at work, supplying a feathery vanilla mattress for peach, butterscotch, cooked pear, caramelized sugars, and honeycomb bars to bounce upon. Soda retains this sweetness, adding extra freesia and hyacinth; ginger is calling out to be made into a Mamie Taylor, and although coconut water and green tea are slightly less successful, both are pleasant mixes. The clincher is cola, where a new layer of red fruits is added, but without any extra dry wood. It works across the board. Job done.

FLAVOUR CAMP	M2	COLA	4
SODA	4	COCONUT WATER	3
GINGER ALE	4	GREEN TEA	3

OBAN 14 YEAR OLD

Citrus is one of the key flavour bridges in whisky, and Oban is so brimming with it that you feel like you've got lost in Mr Tropicana's orchard. It is inescapable, even though baked peaches, nutmeg, and white chocolate all emerge, you always come back to some orange-influenced thing – macerated, jelly, pith, and zest. Soda is very fresh and lively, with a lift of orange blossom, some smoke, and a slight briny tingle on the lips. Green tea flounders, cola's a clash – it's too sweet – but the citrus links well with coconut water. Ginger is an absolute star, takes on that citric intensity, setting sail for Curaçao, trailing light smoke and spice in its wake. The best way to enjoy it.

FLAVOUR CAMP	M2	COLA	2
SODA	4	COCONUT WATER	3
GINGER ALE	5*	GREEN TEA	2

SINGLETON OF DUFFTOWN 12 YEAR OLD

The European exclusive of the Singleton triumvirate is a medium-rich dram where the nutty core of the malt is given some heft by a mix of American and – more overtly – European oak casks, which gives the drinker a mix of Weetabix, Dundee cake, and a slight porridge/white pudding note. Soda is a little too crisp for all of this but is sound enough; green tea is fairly edgy; but coconut water's fatness seems to meld with the malt, adding a light sesame note. Cola is quite pleasant at 1:1 with those figgy elements the key, and ginger works well.

FLAVOUR CAMP	M3	COLA	4
SODA	3	COCONUT WATER	3
GINGER ALE	3	GREEN TEA	2

SINGLETON OF GLENDULLAN 12 YEAR OLD

Although situated a stone's throw away from the Dufftown distillery, the character here for the America/ Latin America Singleton brand is more overtly fruity – with blue fruits (damson, blueberry, sloe) to the front, along with black grape. There's a tingle of acidity when neat, which is encouraging when mixing, and the wood, while on the sherried side again, isn't overly tannic, though having said that, green tea manages to find a nagging clash. Soda and coconut water are both clean, with the former showing a lighter, almost green side, although the impact is a little diminished. Ginger perks up the fruits, revealing raspberry leaf, but cola with added black grape is the most successful.

FLAVOUR CAMP	M3	COLA	4
SODA	3	COCONUT WATER	2
GINGER ALE	4	GREEN TEA	2

SINGLETON OF GLEN ORD 12 YEAR OLD

When you walk into the Glen Ord stillhouse you're immediately baffled at how a freshly cut lawn could be inside. It's this intense grassiness – and light acidity – that gives Glen Ord its heart. In 12-year-old guise this is bulked out with unripe peaches, ginger, toffee, and, in common with Glendullan, a fig note (here green fig jam). It's hard to pick out its smokiness when neat, but is easier with soda, where the grassiness also shows its hand. There's a resistance to green tea (sadly, as this is The Singleton for Asia) and coconut water, but cola provides plummy depth, and ginger goes right into a buttered slice of gingerbread, again with some smoke.

FLAVOUR CAMP	M3	COLA	3
SODA	3	COCONUT WATER	2
GINGER ALE	4	GREEN TEA	2

SPRINGBANK 12 YEAR OLD

Here's a distillery that does things very much its own way: malting, distilling, ageing, and bottling on site – the only place in Scotland to do so. The equipment could be described as "heritage era", the adherence to two-and-a-half times distillation idiosyncratic, but this adherence to its own ways is what has made this a cult malt globally. There's light but ever-present smoke, a hard-to-pin-down mix of black olive, tangerine, sherry, oily fruitiness, and a salty kiss on the finish. It blossoms with water, building in intense waves of flavour. While soda works, its peated sister Longrow is the better bet with that mixer. The rest just quake at Springbank's personality. Drink it, but don't mess with it.

FLAVOUR CAMP	M2/4	COLA	N/A
SODA	N/A	COCONUT WATER	N/A
GINGER ALE	N/A	GREEN TEA	N/A

TALISKER 10 YEAR OLD

The whisky from Skye's sole distillery plays land and shore off each other successfully. It starts with seemingly low levels of smoke, just a few wisps of burning heather behind soft pear that's got brine and dry seaweed added. All seems calm and sweet before a salt-and-pepper blast triggers the smoke. Cola is a mess, but with coconut water we're back to our Brazilian beach bonfire. Green tea goes medicinal but is sweet enough to work. Ginger needs a shorter serve to maximize its impact and bring the smoke out. Soda is the perfect balanced mix here (at 2:1), the smoke and the salinity surging through a storm at sea. Elemental.

FLAVOUR CAMP	M4	COLA	1
SODA	5	COCONUT WATER	3
GINGER ALE	3	GREEN TEA	3

IRISH WHISKEY

The Irish have specialized in making hugely amenable whiskeys for hundreds of years. In fact, when I use "Irish" as a shorthand tasting term for any whiskey it means "ridiculously easy-drinking, with a juicy fruitiness that's like biting into a super-ripe peach".

Although the three distillers represented here make their whiskeys in different ways, this approachable personality is a shared characteristic. That said, you need to appreciate what variation on this theme each brand offers in order to make the ideal mix – and again don't overlook whiskeys that could be considered underwhelming when tried neat.

What all of them needed was a mixer that enhanced this style, adding subtle new elements to it – but never setting itself up in opposition. Green tea didn't provide it; soda was a little too austere. And while the sweetness of cola was fair, coconut water showed real promise. Again though, ginger showed the way.

BUSHMILLS BLACK BUSH

One malt, one grain. You'd think that this would be a recipe for simplicity. Not in the case of Black Bush. There's a cereal undertow to its rich, dark fruitiness, which brings to mind damson jam, peaches, and a lick of liquorice strap. It is perfect neat but mixer-wise, other than green tea (tannin issues) and coconut water (too leathery), it's a good fit. Soda brings out banana, but the thickness on the tongue is retained. Cola and black fruits are a proven hit, and the mix becomes like anise-laced cream sherry. Ginger sees both elements fusing, making a deep, thoughtful drink with a blast of red fruits.

FLAVOUR CAMP	B3	COLA	4
SODA	3	COCONUT WATER	2
GINGER ALE	5*	GREEN TEA	2

BUSHMILLS ORIGINAL

Just like a folk tale, the youngest member of the Bushmills family tends to be overlooked in preference to its richer and older brothers, but it has special properties of its own. Yes, it is light and slightly edgy with a biscuity, cut-grass note, but the palate is longer and softer than the nose suggests. The answer? Mix! Though not with cola, which reminds me of sitting in a field of burned stubble, and though green tea magnifies the sappiness, this is one that works with coconut water where the freshness cuts through, lifting out fruit and flowers. Soda is in your face, effervescent and fresh, while ginger settles down on the palate adding some weight.

FLAVOUR CAMP	B1	COLA	1
SODA	3	COCONUT WATER	4
GINGER ALE	4	GREEN TEA	2

CONNEMARA TURF MÓR

Ireland's only heavily peated malt (at the moment of writing) might have caused a fuss when it first appeared but it is now an established member of the community. Don't be put off by the rubbery note on the neat nose that rises above the sooty, turfy smoke and rolled oats, because a drop of water immediately sweetens everything – ushering in roasted corn, moss, cooked pear, and light spice. That said, while soda works decently, the other mixers simply start brawling with it. No. Connemara is a water-and-ice whiskey.

FLAVOUR CAMP	M4	COLA	1
SODA	3	COCONUT WATER	2
GINGER ALE	2	GREEN TEA	1

JAMESON

Single-handedly reviving a country's whiskey industry cannot just be done by clever marketing; it has to be backed up in the glass. Such is the case with Jameson. Here you see glimmerings of the oily/apple/spice triumvirate of single pot still, but juicy fresh fruits dominate the nose, while the palate has a popping-candy-like liveliness alongside blackcurrant fruit pastilles. Bar an unfortunate clash with green tea it's an exemplary mixer. Soda makes it floral, cola pulls out the oiliness and some supple leather, ginger has a clean freshness where fruits, oak, and dried peach all shine through, while coconut water is rich, tropical, long, medium-sweet, and balanced. Is Brazil ready for the Irish?

FLAVOUR CAMP	B2	COLA	4
SODA	3	COCONUT WATER	5
GINGER ALE	4	GREEN TEA	2

JAMESON 12 YEAR OLD

There's more single pot still in play here – the percentage rises with each expression of Jameson – seen in a distinct upping of the spiced elements (cumin, coriander, turmeric) and a general deepening of the fruits into apricot, cherry, orange, and tinned peaches that cling to the tongue. Great with ice/neat, it struggles with green tea (dries fearsomely), coconut water (soupy), but soda (at 1:1) sees the dry spices of single pot still shining out. Cola is serious and offers sherry and cocoa, while ginger has head-noddingly serious ginger crispness on show, the whiskey restrained but in total control, with orchard fruits and tingling spices on the finish.

FLAVOUR CAMP	B2	COLA	3
SODA	3	COCONUT WATER	2
GINGER ALE	5	GREEN TEA	1

KILBEGGAN

Like Connemara, this is now part of the Beam stable and as it's at the forefront of the firm's foray into the new world of Irish whiskey, it has duly been repackaged and reformulated. What used to be soft, sweet, and charming has become hugely oily, with masses of new oak, an aroma like box-fresh trainers, and an intense smoky, hickory perfume. The effect is a bit like turning The Chieftains into a heavy-metal band. Soda allows the fruit to come through, but the wood is obtrusive; green tea is too strong, but ginger (well-integrated charred notes and gentleness), cola (fat red fruits), and coconut (a little soupy but fine) all show potential.

FLAVOUR CAMP	B2	COLA	3
SODA	2	COCONUT WATER	3
GINGER ALE	4	GREEN TEA	2

REDBREAST 12 YEAR OLD

One of the most welcome happenings in world whisky was the 2011 decision by Irish Distillers to launch its range of single pot still whiskeys. The 12-year-old Redbreast is the most easily found and shows single pot still at its most defiant: oily and rich with stewed plums, light leather, creme caramel, and a dense, raisined palate where the tongue tries to cleave through the white peaches. A whiskey that by the sheer force of its good nature forces you to succumb and accept life on its terms – and that means not trying to mix with it. Redbreast is best on its own.

FLAVOUR CAMP	M3	COLA	N/A
SODA	N/A	COCONUT WATER	N/A
GINGER ALE	N/A	GREEN TEA	N/A

TULLAMORE DEW

Now part of the William Grant stable and with a distillery on the way, the future looks healthy for Tullamore Dew, an Irish brand, which, although a major seller, has always shunned the limelight. Appropriately enough it's pretty green in all departments, quite perfumed with floral grain characters and a light nuttiness. It mixes well with green tea to show its estery side, while ginger ale is a little shy, but pleasant, and although cola fizzles out because of the lack of weight, soda and coconut water work – the former very lively and buttery but the latter transformative. Out of nowhere come basket-loads of pineapple and tropical fruits. A real winner.

FLAVOUR CAMP	B1	COLA	2
SODA	3	COCONUT WATER	5*
GINGER ALE	3	GREEN TEA	3

AMERICAN WHISKEY

The accepted wisdom here is that bourbon and cola is the way to go, and while it was a mix that performed strongly in each flavour camp, binding its sweetness to that of the spirit, it was ginger that was most consistent, with sweetness and spice, and the higher carbonation driving the flavours along the tongue. As with malts, I got the feeling that in many cases, some orange bitters or citrus peel would help balance and elevate the drink to greater heights. Green tea struggled with the high levels of oak extract, while soda tended to be somewhat skeletal, but coconut water acquitted itself well.

The key here was how influential the rye element was. The more rye there was in the whiskey, the tougher things became – making me wonder whether it was this stubbornness that sealed straight rye's fate after Prohibition, when consumers had become used to drinking Canadian rye and ginger.

Rye won't change to suit your requirements, so you have to craft the mixer around it – and simple mixers are just too gentle to be able to force the issue. Neither do you want to tame the rye by heavy dilution. This is the world's most wanton whiskey. I want it to be flaky, and crazy, I want rye to flare and flame. Pass me the vermouth and absinthe...

In conclusion, it is the brand and the flavours of that brand that matter, but if in doubt, go ginger!

BOURBON

BUFFALO TRACE

Although there's no age statement, one sniff of Buffalo Trace shows there's mature stock being used. Rich and complex, there's a bittersweet balance from the start – dessert and Seville orange, cocoa, fresh herbs, pine, and then honeyed corn infused with dark berry fruits. It's the citric element that soda runs with, giving a refreshing mix. Cola latches on to the rich mid-palate, the result is like sucking boiled sweets while drinking cherry cola; coconut pulls out the herbal top notes, though remaining a big drink; green tea sets up in opposition to the oak. Ginger hits the perfect balance, extending aromas into bubblegum, then deepening the layers and ending with a zing of spice. Versatile.

FLAVOUR CAMP	NAM1	COLA	3
SODA	4	COCONUT WATER	4
GINGER ALE	5	GREEN TEA	3

ELIJAH CRAIG 12 YEAR OLD

You're in a venerable Kentucky gentlemen's club here – the lingering scent of cigars, humidor, leather, old spices, wine cellars. Water makes things brighter, with fennel pollen, raspberry, and lots of mint. Elijah's serious nature helps to marry it with soda, though it's a touch dry. Not for the only time, wood is too much for green tea. Cola works – it's those leathery notes – but it ends up as a poor man's Manhattan. Coconut water needs something with more energy. The oak makes ginger become powdery but is very well balanced. Mix if you wish, but it's probably happier as an Old-Fashioned, which seems pretty appropriate.

FLAVOUR CAMP	NAM1	COLA	4
SODA	3	COCONUT WATER	3
GINGER ALE	4	GREEN TEA	2

BOURBON

EVAN WILLIAMS

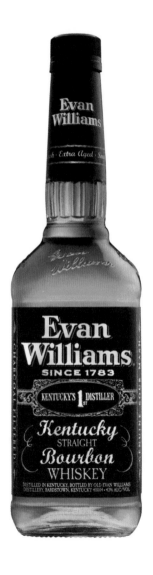

Pull up a chair and settle in by the fire with this relaxed, easy-going, and mellow character. There's a glass of iced coffee, some dark chocolate, caramel toffees, plump cushions, and even when the rye suddenly announces itself, it does so politely. Funny, then, that there's some prickly relationships with mixers: soda has trouble with the oak, as does green tea, and although coconut water is fine, the finish remains a little bitter. Ginger, however, adds its sweetness to the mid-palate and makes this a deep and slow-sipping long drink. The same applies to cola, where liquorice and toffee are brought forward and that pesky oak is kept in check by the sweetness.

FLAVOUR CAMP NAM3		COLA	4
SODA	2	COCONUT WATER	3
GINGER ALE	4	GREEN TEA	1

BOURBON

FOUR ROSES SMALL BATCH

With two mashbills and five yeast strains, Four Roses is set up to create multifaceted bourbons, and while each expression shows different aspects of this base, all share a heightened rye kick. There are lemon oils, sherbet, wild cherry, hints of raspberry vinegar, eucalyptus, and masses of cinnamon. Coconut water and green tea struggle, the former pleasing enough but not enhancing the bourbon, while there's a collapse with the latter. Soda is, again, a little dry but citrus would help and allow the menthol to sing; cola becomes perfumed with added maraschino cherry and charred oak; but ginger shows exemplary balance where intense sparks of spice fly across the tongue adding to a long finish. Complex stuff.

FLAVOUR CAMP NAM3		COLA	4
SODA	2	COCONUT WATER	3
GINGER ALE	5*	GREEN TEA	1

BOURBON

JIM BEAM WHITE LABEL

There's freshness at work here, coming across as zesty grapefruit, spiky ginger with little jags of rye. The palate is slightly softer; here lurk cooked apple and cooling menthol. Everything is very UP. There's not quite enough depth to work with green tea, meaning a clash between wood and tea tannin, although the char adds an interesting burned note to coconut water. Soda is clean (green garden twine) and off-dry; add some lemon for full integration. The dusty rye is pushed forward with ginger – here orange is the key to add some sweetness. Cola has the right balance – the spicy attack cuts through the sweetness, the red fruits in the mixer adding weight. A swaggering afternoon drink.

FLAVOUR CAMP NAM3		COLA	5
SODA	3	COCONUT WATER	3
GINGER ALE	4	GREEN TEA	2

BOURBON

JIM BEAM BLACK LABEL

Older than White Label – this carries an 6-year-old age statement – there's no surprise that you're dealing with a bigger and deeper beast here. There's still some of the green vegetal note adding life, but you soon dip into treacle toffee, char, a little pecan, liquorice, and then rye. That extra oak means that soda and coconut water struggle pushing out the rye and becoming unbalanced, and you know what I'm going to say about green tea. Even cola struggles to maintain its sweetness but there are enough cherry notes to make it work. Ginger is much better: there's still allspice and acidity from the rye, but better balance.

FLAVOUR CAMP NAM3		COLA	3
SODA	2	COCONUT WATER	2
GINGER ALE	4	GREEN TEA	1

BOURBON

MAKER'S MARK

By replacing rye with wheat, Maker's Mark cuts down on spice and acidity, but allows more lifted aromatics to come through. Consequently, this is one of the most scented of bourbons – delicately fruity, with rosemary, rose petal, and cherry blossom. With water it moves into oolong territory, so it's no surprise that green tea works, although you still need sweetness to balance the oak, which even dries cola but adds spice – no bad thing. There's a heightened exoticism at work with Maker's – coconut water takes you down to the seashore: hot sand and gardenia; ginger heads towards Thailand with notes of galangal, basil, and sandalwood.

FLAVOUR CAMP NAM2		COLA	4
SODA	2	COCONUT WATER	3
GINGER ALE	5	GREEN TEA	3

WL WELLER

This is a wheated bourbon that places you in the middle of a balmy southern afternoon. Weller takes things slowly; there's no attack, no surprises on the finish, just a long, gentle story as your eyes slowly close. Baked dessert apple dusted with cinnamon, melting milk chocolate; thick, slow-moving oak, and blueberry jam. It means that soda's starchiness doesn't fit, and ginger's peppiness is a little overexcited. Coconut water drifts by, but green tea's complex aromatic nose is fascinating enough to suggest there's potential here. Cola gets the relaxed vibe, allowing dark fruits to bubble out, but it's an unnecessary drink as water or ice will suffice. Why disturb the afternoon when you can just add a rock of ice?

FLAVOUR CAMP NAM2		COLA	4
SODA	2	COCONUT WATER	3
GINGER ALE	3	GREEN TEA	3

BOURBON

WOODFORD RESERVE

The Labrot & Graham distillery's three pot stills provide some of the make for this sweet and citric bourbon. Waxed lemons, thyme, and apple sit behind huge crème brûlée notes, squished red fruits, and barbecued pineapple drizzled with maple syrup – and there's a light, dusty-rye element on the finish. It matches pretty decently with soda, even if the minerality is a little rigid; ginger starts off with the rye swirling up like a dusty cloud but the storm soon settles back into a relaxed sweet drink. Cola works nicely, accentuating the citrus and soft in the centre. The other two? Not here, I'm afraid. A Manhattan, however...

FLAVOUR CAMP	NAM1	COLA	3
SODA	3	COCONUT WATER	1
GINGER ALE	4	GREEN TEA	1

BOURBON

WILD TURKEY 8 YEAR OLD

As bourbon styles have changed around it, Wild Turkey has stuck to its roots. This is a good ol' boy with heft, punch, and considerable complexity. Sweet, layered black fruits mix with allspice, chestnut honey, sour cherry, and apricot jam. Unctuous, roasted, and crackling with rye, it's a huge mouthful. Soda makes it fragrant and anise-like, but the tethered bear soon strains at the chains. Its sheer amiability rubs along with coconut water, but with cola there's a sense of things massing. Layered and jammy, this has substance. Ginger has extra dimensions: Turkish delight, Moroccan spice – slightly dry to start, deep, and then lingering, an evolving fusion. Listen to the ol' boy; he's got a lot to say.

FLAVOUR CAMP NAM1		COLA	5
SODA	3	COCONUT WATER	4
GINGER ALE	5*	GREEN TEA	1

TENNESSEE WHISKEY

JACK DANIEL'S

The default call of (mostly) young drinkers is "Jack 'n' Coke", but is there more? When neat it's young, fresh, sappy, with pear and apple a-plenty, a decent belt of rye and a sootiness that could come from the charcoal mellowing. In the centre of all this youthful bravado is a still, sweet core. I wouldn't have it neat, nor mix it with too-dry soda, but instead reach for the ginger ale to see the rooty sootiness; or coconut water, where Jack becomes subtle, fresh, and energetic. Green tea, so problematic in Kentucky, finds a home in Tennessee: scented, rounded, and well-balanced. That leaves cola – which, for me, is pretty flat and less impressive. Widen your vision!

FLAVOUR CAMP NAM3		COLA	3
SODA	2	COCONUT WATER	4
GINGER ALE	4	GREEN TEA	4

JACK DANIEL'S GENTLEMAN JACK

With double charcoal mellowing, here we see Jack in a slightly less firm mood, with more sweet oak, slightly less sootiness but a greater rye kick, more candied peels and redcurrant and a final kiss of menthol and green herbs. Strangely, when you add soda you are right next to the charcoal pits, which, while unexpected, are quite pleasant; ginger is lifted and also allows that sooty edge to come through. Coconut is less compelling than with the standard Jack, but once again green tea is lifted aromatically, here into orchard fruits and banana. Unlike its brother, the softer mid-palate allows it to work much more effectively with cola – there are even hints of cigar leaf, ash, and cherry wood.

FLAVOUR CAMP NAM3		COLA	5
SODA	3	COCONUT WATER	3
GINGER ALE	4	GREEN TEA	4

RYE WHISKEY

PIKESVILLE SUPREME

Rye isn't pretty. It's uncompromising, angular, and refuses to bow to fashion. You get what you pay for, which here means a fizzing explosion of dusty spices, lemon oil, and just a little oak. Even though it's sweet to start, the acidic build-up starts early, adding a sour-cherry kiss-off. Soda is a disaster; ginger is like an orchid house, with a headlong charge of spices on the finish; coconut water moves into an interesting Japanese-style sweet-and-sour mode; and while the aromatic nose on green tea gives hope as a straight mix it's a let-down on the palate. It would work as an element in a drink, as would vermouth instead of cola. Uncompromising.

FLAVOUR CAMP NAM3		COLA	3
SODA	1	COCONUT WATER	2
GINGER ALE	4	GREEN TEA	2

RYE WHISKEY

RITTENHOUSE RYE

Clean and intense this may be, but underneath the buzz that greets you on the nose there's real vanilla-led sweetness here, the signature dustiness of American rye given a parma violet edge. Soda again founders, showing its saline side. Cola is pretty peppery, but even it struggles to cope. Coconut water is subtly dry with the spices well balanced, making this a well-mannered drink, but is that what you want? Again, aromatically, green tea has just the right level of sweetness but is one-dimensional in the mouth – there's potential here though. Ginger, while more straight-ahead, is successful: retaining energy and flashing out bitter-lemon notes.

FLAVOUR CAMP NAM3		COLA	3
SODA	1	COCONUT WATER	3
GINGER ALE	4	GREEN TEA	3

RYE WHISKEY

SAZERAC RYE

Here's a more serious rye. More age has added integrated oak, making it sweeter and slightly deeper, but not at the expense of intensity. Here the rye is cut with nutmeg, clove, and allspice. The palate is a fluxing mix of the sweet and sour, the buttery and the tart, but all in perfect balance. There's a glimmer of hope for soda, but it's quickly closed down; green tea perks up on the nose with lots of banana, but dries rapidly; coconut water kicks off fruity, but ends up like an ashtray; even ginger, while showing perfectly compatible elements, ends aggressively. Cola is the only one not to lose any impact, but Sazerac is best in a Sazerac... *quelle surprise*!

FLAVOUR CAMP NAM3		COLA	4
SODA	1	COCONUT WATER	3
GINGER ALE	3	GREEN TEA	2

CANADIAN WHISKY

Despite the volume sold, Canadian whisky remains an underappreciated style. Because of Prohibition, its brands have been misinterpreted as rye, whereas they mostly only contain a small amount of rye whisky in the blend (that said, there is the Canadian equivalent of a straight rye here).

In America, they're seen as being the same as straight bourbon, with different mashbills giving the variety of flavours, whereas they are blends of different flavouring whiskies.

While rye has long been used to give a kick to the blend, it is the corn base that is the key to this style – its sweetness is central to understanding Canadian whisky. Importantly, Canadian distillers can reuse casks, so that although American oak barrels are the most common type used, there is a scaling back of the big vanilla/coconut/pine notes you get in bourbon. This more subtle oak allows the character of the blend to show. Think of honeycombed sweetness, light spice, plenty of fruit. As with Scotch blends, here whiskies routinely dismissed when encountered neat leaped to life when put with a mixer. Ginger ale was the most successful, green tea variable, cola fair, soda a little too austere but coconut water mix was very consistent.

ALBERTA PREMIUM DARK HORSE

Canadian whisky has often been called rye, when the reality is that there is often only a small percentage of that grain in the mashbill. This, my friends, is Canadian rye, a rip-snorting mix of 12-year-old and 6-year-old pot still with just sufficient corn whisky to give a soft landing. As the name suggests it's on the dark side: tayberry, prune, sloe, black cherry, cassis with a backing of ras-el-hanout spiciness. Charred barrels add a smoky vanilla touch. Aromatic and powerful, it's a sleek horse that paws the ground and tramples all mixers into the dust. I'd leave this fantastic whisky on its own, or try it as a boulevardier or sazerac.

FLAVOUR CAMP NAM3		COLA	1
SODA	3	COCONUT WATER	1
GINGER ALE	2	GREEN TEA	2

BLACK VELVET

From Lethbridge in the Albertan prairie, the Black Velvet distillery is a corn specialist amidst fields of wheat and rye and is a far more civilized place than the first whisky-related outpost in the vicinity, the infamous Indian trading post Fort Whoop-Up. These days it is Americans who buy Black Velvet – the distillery was built in 1973 to satisfy demand in the western states. Lush corn is to the fore, with caramelized apple, lime, raspberry, caramel toffee, and a discreet jag of rye. A good rocks blend, it's fair if dry at 1:1 with soda, though cola bludgeons its charms, and green tea, while pleasant, is a little nondescript. Coconut water adds a deliciously sweet, buttery richness; ginger ale brings out an orange-peel element alongside mint and a peppy finish. I prefer it at 1:1, where the gentle character is maximized.

FLAVOUR CAMP NAM1		COLA	2
SODA	3	COCONUT WATER	4
GINGER ALE	4	GREEN TEA	3

CANADIAN CLUB

Almost by default, Canadian whiskies became cocktail bases during Prohibition and were the base for the era's favourite speakeasy call of "Rye and ginger". Foremost among them was Canadian Club. Front-loaded with dusty spices and hints of green apple, it becomes loquaciously smooth on the tongue, where soft corn rules. Soda is the only disappointment here; cola adds weight and links with vanilla, but needs lime; coconut is an enhanced mix – vinous, fruity, lightly citric – while ginger simply works: crackling, fresh, fennel-like, with balanced sweetness. Green tea, though, is an unexpected star, a gorgeous mix of just enough fragrance, sweetness, dryness, and spice while still being pure and clean. A whisky made for mixing.

FLAVOUR CAMP	NAM1	COLA	4
SODA	2	COCONUT WATER	4
GINGER ALE	5	GREEN TEA	5 *

CANADIAN CLUB CLASSIC 12 YEAR OLD

Although this is a Canadian Club with its malted barley element upped, it's the use of re-charred casks that is immediately apparent, with coconut, pine, cassia, and ginger added to the flambéed banana and treacle toffee before rye takes charge, with sourdough notes mixed with mace, cinnamon, and fenugreek. Water brings out plummy fruit. Cola makes things go weird and bitter. Green tea falls by the wayside, and while coconut water is in charge, the combination is softly seductive. Ginger links with the rye, but needs to be at 2:1 for the fruits to re-emerge. It's the reverse for soda, however, where a serve of equal parts permits flavours to deepen and stops the rye becoming dusty.

FLAVOUR CAMP NAM3		COLA	1
SODA	4	COCONUT WATER	3
GINGER ALE	3	GREEN TEA	2

CROWN ROYAL

I can't help thinking of honey-bear jars when I stick my nose into a glass of Crown Royal. It's so huge and sweet with crème brûlée and heady, jammy red and black fruits, but then comes new wood, spice, and orange zest. Okay, it's always going to be more skewed towards caramel fudge sauce, but there's enough drying rye to maintain a balance. The sweetness means soda is way too dry, as is green tea. Coconut water provides red fruit, while ginger pulls out the fruit syrups and links with the rye, adding drive to the finish. Counter-intuitively, cola also picks out the rye, making this less of a sugar bomb than you might expect. The honey bear has teeth.

FLAVOUR CAMP	NAM1	COLA	4
SODA	2	COCONUT WATER	3
GINGER ALE	3	GREEN TEA	2

CROWN ROYAL RESERVE

This starts as a more serious proposition than the standard Crown Royal, with greater wood influence and mature stock: crème brûlée, hints of sherry, cassia bark, and blackberry with a sprig of mint adding a top note. The palate is fat with overripe mango and is so sweet that initially it's like being assaulted by Barbies before you're saved by lemon-accented rye and toasty oak. That wood is too obtrusive with green tea and cola, and coconut water is fruity, but no better than okay. Best to keep things traditional with soda, which gently enhances the rye. Ginger ale provides a rich and quite sweet palate, but the double-spice combo stops things from becoming too flabby.

FLAVOUR CAMP	NAM1	COLA	2
SODA	4	COCONUT WATER	3
GINGER ALE	4	GREEN TEA	1

FORTY CREEK DOUBLE BARREL RESERVE

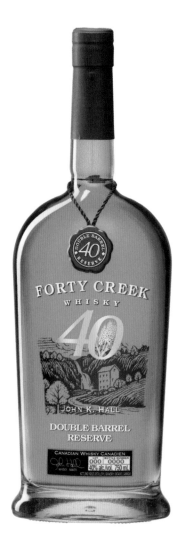

A blend of separately aged corn, rye, and malt whiskies given second maturation in ex-bourbon barrels – this is so proudly Canadian that the first thing on the nose is maple syrup, quickly followed by pine, coconut, and cherry. The palate is an ever-shifting dance between the different elements: chewy sweetness from corn, dry cereal from malt, and the lemon of rye. It thickens then dries, spices up, then sweetens. All very hospitable, but there's little to make green tea, coconut water, or cola compelling mixes – they either dominate or jostle the whisky into uncomfortable areas. Ginger, however, adds lift and floral fragrance, while soda pulls out mint, waxiness, spices, and a tingling, zesty finish. Serious but also easy-going.

FLAVOUR CAMP NAM1		COLA	3
SODA	4	COCONUT WATER	3
GINGER ALE	4	GREEN TEA	2

GIBSON'S STERLING

Rarely seen outside of its homeland, this is a whisky that comes across as shy after the big sweethearts of the rodeo, which also exist in Canada's camp. Everything here is poised: the wood gives grip, the rye is understated, the corn while chewy isn't too fat and flabby. Instead you get red cherry, citrus, and berry fruits. It plumps out with water, showing good energy. Soda makes it collapse, while cola gives it a nervous breakdown. Green tea is a little dry, but there are positive perfumed notes. It's coconut water that allows the whisky's finesse to show best alongside apple and orange. Ginger needs to be at 1:1 to strike the best balance. A class act.

FLAVOUR CAMP	NAM1	COLA	2
SODA	2	COCONUT WATER	4
GINGER ALE	4	GREEN TEA	3

SEAGRAM'S VO

VO is seen as no more than a mixing whisky, but the point of mixing whiskies is to make compelling drinks. Fair enough, it's not hugely complex, but there's enough mashed-banana softness to charm on the nose, sufficient steely rye to show there's an edge. This hard element clashes with soda and green tea, but the other mixers transform this humble whisky. Ginger is the classic, adding spice, bending the steel to its sweet/spicy will; cola pulls out rye and adds energy, it's a Canadian Cubata; and while you expect everything to get sweeter with coconut water, instead it goes dry, roasted and toasty, the rye slotting underneath, the sweetness flowing through. That's what a mixing whisky is all about.

FLAVOUR CAMP	NAM3	COLA	5
SODA	2	COCONUT WATER	5*
GINGER ALE	4	GREEN TEA	2

WISER'S DELUXE

There is something so comfortable about Wiser's Deluxe. It leads with rye but does so in an extremely well-mannered fashion, mixing in sandalwood, blonde tobacco, mace, and fennel seed sitting on top of red apples and honeyed oak. Again, soda is a disaster but all of the others are welcomed into its gentle warmth. Ginger picks up real complexity with added limey verve, and though cola is more of a smouldering brunette, it has depth, which overwhelms any blowsy sweetness. Coconut water is leading the dance with lush fruits, while green tea is lightly herbal but needs another element to give it more lift. All in all, Mr Wiser is your friend, your shoulder to cry on, Canada's Mr Reliable.

FLAVOUR CAMP NAM3		COLA	5
SODA	1	COCONUT WATER	4
GINGER ALE	5	GREEN TEA	3

JAPANESE & TAIWANESE WHISKY

Japan is where, as far as mature markets are concerned, whisky was rebooted by the Highball, so you would imagine that all of the mixes should have worked. As there was a pretty small sample it would be wrong to draw grand conclusions. Better instead to look at how the Japanese way of making whisky influenced how they performed. Japan may make its whiskies in the same way as the Scots, but some subtle differences in production and more significant changes in climate help to give them their own individuality.

One of these production aspects influences single malts. The two largest distillers, Suntory and Nikka, do not exchange stock as happens in Scotland for blending. Instead, they make a wide number of styles at each of their sites. Their single malts are a "blend" of a number of these styles – completely different to Scotch, where a single character is promoted. This approach, allied to a Japanese clarity of character and precision of aroma, conceivably assists with a seamless, flowing quality shared by blends and malts alike. Quite different to Scotch.

HIBIKI 12 YEAR OLD

The surprise element in the newest member of the Hibiki range comes just as you have been seduced by its calm, complex charms, a seamless mix of red fruits, chocolate brownie, fruit sugars, and an oozingly soft palate. Just as you are swooning, in comes a fresh jab of acidity from whisky aged in casks that have held Japanese plum wine. Every taste covered. Like all great blends, the mixer shows different facets of the whisky: with soda it's fruit blossom; ginger, exotic spices like long pepper and cumin; cola is velvety dried plum; green tea incense and wood; while coconut water is a major revelation, boosting the jellied fruits and adding roasted notes. A great all-rounder.

FLAVOUR CAMP	B2	COLA	4
SODA	4	COCONUT WATER	5
GINGER ALE	5	GREEN TEA	3

JAPANESE BLENDS

KAKUBIN

Kaku has had two lives – as the blend that started Japanese whisky culture in 1937 and rebooted it in 2009. It's a clever blend, which has Japanese clarity of aroma, restrained appley fruits, a creamily soft palate, but with added crispness of roasted nuts and dry reeds. It's this dry finish that makes you take another sip, preferably with soda. Sure, coconut water moves it into a bamboo-like area; cola makes it sweet and earthy; and though ginger dominates, green tea has superb balance and layers of flavours. But it's soda that wins: fresh, clean, dry, with just enough sweetness from the Kaku. Lively, refreshing, and what you need after a long day's work – with a lemon twist.

FLAVOUR CAMP	B1	COLA	3
SODA	5*	COCONUT WATER	3
GINGER ALE	2	GREEN TEA	4

NIKKA FROM THE BARREL

It's to do with mass. The bottle is small and square, the alcohol high, giving an overall effect of something compressed, like a star that's collapsing. Here's a strong (51.3% ABV) blend for the serious drinker, but which has such concentrated flavours (bitter chocolate, prune, smoke, dried mango) that the alcohol doesn't burn. It does, however, require careful matching: ginger picks up smoke, cola and green tea both clash with the tannins, but coconut water holds its own, adding new freshness. Soda is our friend, revealing hidden fragrant top notes, retaining the fruity depths, tickling the finish with smoke. Or just light a cigar and have it with water and an ice ball.

FLAVOUR CAMP	B3	COLA	3
SODA	5	COCONUT WATER	3
GINGER ALE	3	GREEN TEA	3

JAPANESE GRAIN WHISKY

NIKKA COFFEY GRAIN

NIKKA
COFFEY GRAIN
WHISKY

PRODUCED BY THE NIKKA WHISKY
DISTILLING CO., LTD., JAPAN

カフェグレーン

alc.45%   ウイスキー   500ml
NIKKA WHISKY

Grain used to be dismissed by whisky aficionados who believed it was just neutral alcohol that diluted flavour-packed single malts. Then whiskies such as this revealed the truth. It's a dessert on a desert island – banana split, raspberry jam, toffee, lime, papaya, custard. Light dilution brings out dusty cinnamon. Soda kills this unctuous nature, cola obliterates it, but ginger enhances the finish and adds lemon-oil smoothness. With green tea there's frangipani flowers in the mid-palate. But it's made for a tropical mixer, and when put with coconut water, the two elements slide around each other, never too sweet, or too dry, just a fusion of fruit, coffee, and butterscotch syrup. Sensual.

FLAVOUR CAMP	B2	COLA	2
SODA	3	COCONUT WATER	5*
GINGER ALE	4	GREEN TEA	4

HAKUSHU 12 YEAR OLD

Fresh, cool, and reserved, Hakushu is a melange of basil, mint, green tea, bamboo, mint, grape, melon, apple, and pine trees with wisps of smoke drifting through them. If ever there were a green whisky, this would be it. It doesn't take a genius to work out that cola's forcefulness won't work here; the rest, however, do. Ginger slides in beside the whiskey's pure, transparent nature and produces an effect like a Thai green curry in a glass; coconut water needs to be COLD to allow the bamboo elements to come through; soda is like an appetizing Basil Julep (and that smoke is important), while green tea is very subtle, posed, and harmonious – but that's Hakushu.

FLAVOUR CAMP	M1	COLA	1
SODA	4	COCONUT WATER	3
GINGER ALE	3	GREEN TEA	4

YAMAZAKI 12 YEAR OLD

The first purpose-built whisky distillery in Japan, Yamazaki produces a wide range of different characters aged in different wood types and then blended together to widen complexity. At 12, its palate-clinging fruitiness has added polish, dried orange peel, dry reeds/tatami, barley sugar, vanilla, and zesty spice on the finish. What's surprising is how tricky it becomes with mixers. There's just too much wood for green tea, the fruits are lost with soda, and cola is clumsy. Coconut water is good, if a little obvious, leaving ginger to fly. Here we have ginger root adding a frisson to the mid-palate and linking with the fruits.

FLAVOUR CAMP	M2	COLA	2
SODA	2	COCONUT WATER	3
GINGER ALE	4	GREEN TEA	2

JAPANESE MALT WHISKY

YAMAZAKI 18 YEAR OLD

While this expression shares Yamazaki's fruity core, there is less of the pineapple and more of the depth here – evidence of more mature stock, but also more powerful distillates (remember that each Japanese single malt is a different amalgamation of whisky types produced at the distillery). The most obvious addition is an upping of *mizunara* (Japanese oak) in this mix, adding incense to the melange of ripe apple, violet, strawberry jam, dark chocolate, and deep, sweet oakiness. There are dried autumn fruits: semi-dried peach, raisin, and added walnut, date, and molasses showing a higher percentage of sherry casks as well. Mixing is an unnecessary exercise with this. All that's required is an ice ball, or some chilled water on the side – and a Cohiba Maduro cigar, if that takes your fancy.

FLAVOUR CAMP	M3	COLA	N/A
SODA	N/A	COCONUT WATER	N/A
GINGER ALE	N/A	GREEN TEA	N/A

JAPANESE MALT WHISKY

YOICHI 15 YEAR OLD

Located on Hokkaido's western coast, Yoichi has retained a belief in the old, weighty ways: peated malt, coal-fired stills, worm tubs. Surprisingly, with this example what you first encounter is the opposite: apple, candy, hints of smoked tea, mixing with potpourri and strawberry. Then you add water and out comes the sooty, creosote-like oiliness. It's forceful, sweet, heavy, and brimming with such cussed individuality that mixers crumble before it. With ginger it's oily and salty, it pushes cola out of the way after a hint of sandalwood, while green tea – even with the lapsang souchong hit – just picks up tannins. Soda works the best – the smoke thing again – but you do need lemon. It's probably best to have it with water.

FLAVOUR CAMP	M4	COLA	2
SODA	4	COCONUT WATER	2
GINGER ALE	3	GREEN TEA	2

TAIWANESE MALT WHISKY

KAVALAN CLASSIC

A whisky matured in sub-tropical climes is different to one matured in Scotland because of the rapid uptake of oak, but though Kavalan is "young" in Scottish terms, it isn't simply a mix of oak and spirit. In fact, it reflects its home astonishingly accurately, as sweet, tropical fruits, orchid, and frangipani combine with vanilla and coconut. As a short drink, soda has weight, the mixer introducing a sweet, green-olive note; ginger goes floral with some toffee, and while cola is aggressive, coconut at low dilution is like a lemon-spiked whisky Malibu. Most heartening is how it works with green tea, where fruit and flowers are enhanced. A light oolong is even better. It's comfortable. It's at home.

FLAVOUR CAMP	M2	COLA	2
SODA	4	COCONUT WATER	3
GINGER ALE	4	GREEN TEA	5

WHISKY & FOOD

If you sit down with friends to a meal in Taiwan, the likelihood is that the liquid accompaniment will be a bottle of Scotch whisky, served throughout your feast with ice and water. The same could happen across Asia or in Latin America. It would have been commonplace in Scotland in the 19th century (maybe without the ice, however). The idea that whisky cannot be drunk with food is therefore another misconception.

FIND THE PERFECT MATCH

Drinking whisky with a meal is, however, different to whisky being the perfect match for food. That necessitates some deeper thinking, with specific flavours and textures being examined to try and find a perfect equilibrium.

The whisky dinner has become a popular way for whisky firms to try and widen people's understanding of the drink. Having a different dram with each course brings whisky into the dining experience, showing that it can be a valid alternative to wine or beer.

That said, because of its stronger flavour, whisky can be unforgiving. Its higher strength also frequently necessitates dilution – often more than you would consider when simply drinking. The reason is to bring the intensity of the flavour down to the same level as the food.

Most of the work has concentrated on matching single malts with different foods. When they work the pairing can be miraculous, but I'm increasingly of the view that a top-end blend offers a more amenable and easier-to-match option.

This is a fascinating area, albeit one that can become somewhat contrived and proscriptive, which is well worth exploring, but one that is beyond the space available in this book.

Here instead are some personal sure-fire winners that bring whisky into the beginning and end of a meal.

Whisky & Seafood
Because of their light salinity (not to mention their smokiness) peaty single malts work

brilliantly with oysters, lobster, clams, mussels, scallops, and so on. Pairing one with smoked fish, however, is a bit too obvious – go instead for a soft, fruity malt or blend. High-rye-content bourbon or Canadian whisky also works nicely with smoked fish.

Whisky & Sashimi/Sushi
It might seem unlikely, but this can be a devastatingly good combination. Sushi is a package of quite powerful flavours. Seaweed's marine saltiness, the sweet/sour elements in the rice, soy's brewed notes, wasabi's heat, ginger's sweet spice. That's each of the five tastes. Then there's the varying textures and subtle tastes of sashimi – buttery, floral, oozing, firm. No surprise that there are links between the complexities at work here and the complexities within whisky. Too much oak is a killer, though, meaning that sherried malts and bourbons do not work. Instead go for lightly smoked malts, or whiskies with vanilla, fresh fruits, or sweet spice.

Whisky & Chocolate
Wine's acidity and tannin are accepted as reasons why it is a tricky pairing with chocolate. Wood-aged spirits, however, are made for it. This is because the higher alcohol breaks down the fats in the chocolate and allows its highly complex aromas and tastes to be revealed fully. It's not that surprising a partnership when you consider that among chocolate's many aromas are vanilla, cocoa, black fruits, forest floor, and tobacco – all common within whisky. Again lots of oak and tannin don't work.

Whisky & Cheese
This is another pairing where wine struggles – for the same reasons as with chocolate – and where whisky proves a winner, again for the breaking down of fat by higher alcohol, revealing hidden flavours. In addition, the sweetness that balances good whisky is pulled out by the cheese, making the spirit's complexities more apparent.

Whisky also contains a number of key flavours that are not found in wine but are replicated in cheese: grassiness, fermented notes, leather, apple... even salt. The briny note in many coastal whiskies acts as a flavour bridge between the spirit and strong blue cheese. Soft sheep's cheeses are best with fruity whiskies with an American oak influence and while goat's cheese can be tricky, ripe Cheddar is perfectly matched with fresh, apple-like drams. Stilton works with fruity whiskies and smoky ones, and ripe blue cheeses are best with smoky malts.

COCKTAILS

I remember, just over a decade ago, helping to organize a whisky cocktail competition for Whisky Live in London, the final of which was held at the show. As we sat in a judge-like huddle in front of the bar, I could feel the stares from the whisky-lovers in the room boring into my back, I could sense eyebrows being raised and heads being shaken, barely concealed tuts and mutters. It was obvious that to them, this was WRONG. How things have changed. As the world has woken up to whisky, so it has embraced the whisky cocktail.

SIMPLE SYRUP

Gently heat the same amounts of white sugar and water until the sugar has completely dissolved. You can flavour the syrup by adding mint, citrus, and so on.

Or buy a bottle of gomme.

SHAKE, RATTLE & ROLL: THE WHISKY WAY

Cocktails were less of a leap for bourbon, which has always been seen as a spirit that was "allowed" to be mixed into a serious short, cold, hard concoction. It was to prove more problematic for Scotch because of assumptions that had grown up around the style. Not only was it a drink that shouldn't be mixed, it was a drink that couldn't be mixed – a line taken by American writers in the onwards. That's quite a barrier to experimentation.

Probably the only thing that Charles H Baker gets wrong in his remarkable 1939 book *Jigger, Beaker, & Glass* is his statement, "Scotch is not a happy cocktail mixer, unfortunately, and its main value is in a highball called 'whiskysoda' around the civilized and uncivilized world." Little had changed in the 10 years between this and the appearance of David A Embury's *The Fine Art of Mixing Drinks*, where the great man writes: "[Scotch] whisky is a grouchy old bachelor that stubbornly insists on maintaining its own independence and is seldom to be found in the marrying mood."

Now call it stubborn Caledonian pride, but I find this hard to believe. Maybe Scotch blends were different in those days – and it does seem to be smoke that irritates the American writers of this era the most. While it's true that smoke can be too forceful in some drinks, its equally true that not all blends are smoky (nor were they when this propaganda was being written). Scotch has different flavours to bourbon, as do Canadian or Irish whiskies, but that doesn't mean that you cannot tweak a recipe or find a mix that works.

As we'll see later, today's bartenders are starting to embrace Scotch with all of its problems and showing that it isn't grouchy or unhappy, but the opposite. Smoke is no longer a barrier, but an asset; big flavours are positive; an open mind is encouraged. Bartenders are today's arbiters of taste. Their work with all whisky cocktails will ensure a healthy future for the drink.

This is not something confined to the professional. Anyone with a few essentials – shaker, ice, whisky (!), bitters, and a small supporting cast can make fantastic, eye-opening classic whisky drinks at home. It is how it has always been done.

All that needs to be remembered is that you must understand your brand. Most classic recipes simply say "whisky", but that's a bit like saying, "Serve this dish with wine." The key to any successful mixed drink is to bring the main ingredient's personality out. The whisky is an active participant, it sits in the centre and dictates how the other ingredients perform.

The key is balance. By understanding the whisky that you are using you can tweak the recipes to suit the brand and your palate. It's pretty much common sense. Take the Manhattan (*see* pp.190–1). If you have a lighter bourbon – Maker's Mark, for example – you will need to pull the vermouth element back to prevent it being bludgeoned to death. Conversely, heavier bourbons, like Wild Turkey, or straight ryes are balanced when the ratio of vermouth is pushed up – sometimes close to equal proportions. The same applies when you are using Scotch to make a Rob Roy (*see* p.191). Not all brands work. A Rob Roy made with Laphroaig 10 year old is hideous, but with Lagavulin 16 year old (at 2:1) it is sensational. Understand the brand.

Don't forget the bitters. Many of the classics use Angostura, but often it's there because, when the drink was created, it was the only bitters available. Today, there are more bitters than you could ever imagine and these tiny drops of concentrated flavour can bring your drink to life. If you were to choose three to have at home I'd make them Angostura, Peychaud's, and orange.

Whisky is bold in flavour. These are big drinks. Don't expect them to offer nothing but bland alcohol (vodka) or an aromatic lift (gin). Whisky has an edge, it has punch, it has flavour, it has individuality and character. When you put it in a cocktail you get a Whisky Drink. Accept and understand that and fun will be had.

FLAVOURED WHISKIES

HIGHLAND CORDIAL

1 pint whitecurrants (destalked)

peel (no pith) of 1 lemon

½ tsp ginger paste

whisky

Place the whitecurrants, lemon peel, and ginger paste in a bottle and top up with whisky (I use Cutty Sark). Mix and leave for 48 hours. Strain and adjust with sugar to taste. Leave for a further week.

CARAWAY WHISKY

2 pieces of bitter orange peel

30g (1oz) caraway seeds

½ cinnamon stick

whisky

Place the orange peel, caraway seeds, and cinnamon in a bottle and top up with whisky (I use Glenmorangie The Original). Seal and leave for 2 weeks and taste. The caraway is picked up quickly and can give a slightly bitter taste if left for too long. Adjust with an orange-infused simple syrup (see p.185) to taste.

Home-flavouring whisky was common practice in Scotland and, though the practice has seemingly died out, it's something that should be revived. It's a simple – and intuitive – process. The following have all been tried at home and can be recommended. I advise using a light or fruity whisky, and one without smoke. These were all adapted from F Marian MacNeill's *The Scots Cellar* (1956) but many of the recipes predate that by 100 years.

GEAN WHISKY

Gean is Scots for wild cherry. This is a good substitute for cherry brandy.

450g (1lb) cherries, stoned

1 nutmeg

1 blade of mace

5 peppercorns

1 tbsp sugar

whisky

Crush the cherry stones. Place the pulp and stones in a bottle along with the nutmeg, mace, peppercorns, and sugar. Top up with whisky (I use Cutty Sark or Dewar's White Label). Seal. Taste after 2 weeks and adjust with sugar if necessary. The longer the maceration, the more almondy the taste.

HIGHLAND BITTERS

Used as a tonic in the Highlands in the 19th century, while this wakes the senses up I'd leave it for cocktail use only.

15g (½oz) juniper berries

3 cardamom seeds

5g (⅛oz) coriander seeds

1g (1/25oz) dried gentian root

5g (⅛oz) dried calamus root

5g (⅛oz) dried liquorice root

peel from a Seville orange

Crush the juniper, cardamom, and coriander and mix with the root and peel. Place in a bottle and top up with whisky (I use Cutty Sark). Taste daily. Cut down on the gentian or adjust with a small amount of sugar to reduce the bitterness.

RECIPE

One sip and you can see why this easy and refreshing drink became the preferred way of drinking blended Scotch. When it works, it's a serve that enhances the flavour of the whisky, slakes the thirst, and can be consumed over a longer period of time than a shot.

The best serve for me is the one perfected at Rockfish in Tokyo, the cradle of Japan's Highball revolution. Here, the glasses and the whisky (Kakubin) are kept in the freezer – giving the Kaku a thick texture – and the soda is from the fridge, so there is no need for ice. As you get a bigger belt of the whisky, the ratio is 1 whisky:3 soda. A lemon peel is then spritzed on the surface.

It's the bubbles that make this drink interesting, so use tall glasses to preserve them – and to enhance the aroma. The recipe below is my preferred ratio, but it can be made 1:1 if you want more of a belt, or 1:3 for a more soothing effect.

3 ice cubes

1 part whisky

2 parts mixer

Place the ice cubes in a Highball glass. Pour the whisky into the glass. Stir gently. Top with the mixer.

THE HIGHBALL

The Highball started life not with whisky, but with brandy when, thanks to the invention of "charged water" by Joseph Priestley in 1767, it became a highly acceptable drink for Victorian gentlemen. It was then given greater pep with the invention of the soda syphon (see pp.62–3).

Cognac was the first great aged spirit to be mixed, but when phylloxera devastated the region's vineyards production stopped. A substitute was needed. After all, a chap had to drink something. And so, up stepped whisky. Cognac's disappearance also neatly coincided with the arrival of the golden generation of Scotch blenders who transformed what had been a quirky northern product into a global player (see p.31). A squirt of soda made blended Scotch an acceptable middle-class drink around the world. It became ubiquitous.

Quite who was the first to mix a Highball remains a matter of conjecture. A New York bartender called Patrick Duffy claimed that, in 1894, he was the first to mix Highballs at the request of a British actor, EJ Ratcliffe. After acquiring some Usher's blended Scotch, he claimed that, "In a week I sold little but Scotch Highballs... Shortly afterward every actor along Broadway, and consequently every New Yorker who frequented the popular bars, was drinking Scotch Highballs." According to Duffy, it was Ratcliffe who named the drink, but we only have the self-promoting barkeep's word for this.

Was it a British invention? Cocktail historian David Wondrich has uncovered a 1884 reference to a rye and ginger ale Highball with the splendid name of The Splificator, which predates Duffy's claim, so maybe honours are even.

VARIATIONS

MORNING GLORY FIZZ

I tried this (shamefully) for the first time in 2012 when it was agitated for me by David Wondrich. As a picker-upper it is unsurpassed.

3ml (⅛fl oz) Vieux Pontarlier absinthe
3ml (⅛fl oz) water
7.5ml (¼fl oz) freshly squeezed lemon juice, strained
10ml (⅓fl oz) freshly squeezed lime juice, strained
10ml (⅓fl oz) (by vol) sugar
60ml (2fl oz) Blended Scotch
7.5 ml (¼fl oz) egg white
60ml (2fl oz) chilled soda water

Mix the absinthe, water, lemon juice, lime juice, and sugar in a shaker and stir until the sugar has dissolved. Add the whisky and egg white and stir to incorporate. Add ice and shake viciously. To serve, pour into a Highball glass and top off with soda.
(With thanks to David Wondrich)

MAMIE TAYLOR

The drink of the informed bibulator between 1899 and 1902. Quite why it fell from grace is a mystery. You could use ginger ale, but ginger beer has more depth and kick.

60ml (2fl oz) Scotch
22ml (¾fl oz) lime juice
ginger beer
lime wedge, to garnish

In a Highball glass with ice cubes stir together the Scotch and lime juice. Top up with ginger beer and garnish with a lime wedge.
(With thanks to Ted Haigh)

Splificators (aka rye and ginger) were the most popular drinks in Prohibition times, and when America went sensible in the 1950s it was the Scotch Highball that ruled. So closely associated was the "dash and a splash" with Scotch that, when it began to struggle in the late 1970s, the Highball went with it. No surprise, however, that now whisky is back, drinkers are looking at this simplest of mixed drinks afresh.

RECIPE

60ml (2fl oz) bourbon

30ml (1fl oz) sweet vermouth

2-3 dashes of bitters (try a mix of orange and Angostura)

maraschino cherry, to garnish

Stir over ice. Strain into a chilled cocktail glass and garnish with a maraschino cherry.

THE MANHATTAN

The Manhattan is not only the greatest whisky drink; it is, I believe, the ur-cocktail, and as such is the fountainhead of modern mixed drinks.

According to legend it was "invented" in 1874 at the Manhattan Club in New York City for Jennie Jerome (Winston Churchill's mother). There is absolutely no evidence for this. The good burghers of Astoria claim that it was created at the Trafford Mansion in Hallet's Cove by Long Islanders waiting for the ferry to Manhattan. Again, nothing more than idle speculation. Maybe it was invented by a mysterious barkeep called Black who had a tavern on Broadway. Possible, but where's the beef?

The Manhattan Club seems to be the agreed place, but there is no date in the club's records as to when the first example was stirred. What we can say, however, is that it was the first drink to mix hard liquor – probably rye initially – with vermouth. When bartenders began to take this principle and play with other spirits they started by replicating them in a Manhattan style – i.e. they were sweet drinks, which means that the Martini was a gin Manhattan before it morphed into the cocktail we know now.

These two cocktail classics have a strange symbiotic relationship. The easiest way to understand what the Manhattan is to first understand what it isn't, by thinking of the Martini and imagining the opposite.

It's the anti-Martini, whose flavour is a polar opposite to its skeletally pure half-sister. The Manhattan is a *noir* cocktail. It has the hue (and taste) of faded red velvet, the cherry glowing like a jab of red neon in the glass. It's a night-time drink for outsiders. The Manhattan is about maximizing flavour, where the richness of the spirit

VARIATIONS

The simplest way to twist it further is by adding dashes of liqueur (Chartreuse, Gran Marnier, Bénédictine, curaçao, absinthe, and so on), or you can try different vermouth styles; only dry or split equally between dry and sweet to give the (erroneously named, in my mind) Perfect. A Brooklyn (*see* p.204) takes this base and adds in maraschino and Amer Picon.

If you use Scotch as the base, then the drink is called a Rob Roy, and for me it's best dashed with orange bitters. Blends from the B1 camp (*see* p.70) need 2 parts whisky:½ part vermouth; B2 is best at 2:¾; B3 at close to equal parts and B4 2:1½. Don't bother with heavily sherried malts, but Glenfiddich 15 year old works splendidly at 2:1½. You can spin this with dashes of liqueur to make a Bobby Burns (*see* p.209), or again split the vermouth ratio into equal parts sweet and dry to get the Affinity (*see* p.209). For me, lighter and drier Scotches are better in Bobby Burns mode.

melds with the dense herbal sweetness of the vermouth and the exotic spike given by the bitters.

To hit the perfect sultry balance you need to pay attention to the ratio. Vermouth is a big flavour that can easily dominate proceedings. Remember, this is a whiskey drink, not a vermouth drink. Keep that in mind and it's logical. For heavier bourbons, the ratio can be upped to 2:1¾; straight rye is 2:1, while for wheated and light, 2:½ is best.

Try different vermouths. I go for Noilly Prat Rouge, but for the bigger bourbons Carpano Antica Formula can work, but again, play around with the ratio.

RECIPE

60ml (2fl oz) whisky

30ml (1fl oz) lemon juice

15ml (½fl oz) simple syrup or gomme (*see* p.185)

dash of Angostura bitters (optional)

half slice of orange, to garnish

Shake hard over ice and strain into a chilled glass. Garnish with half a slice of orange. A dash of Angostura is an optional extra.

VARIATIONS

Riffing on the Sour theme is easy (that's why it's the largest cocktail family) and usually starts by replacing the sugar with a liqueur or a syrup. Then you can play around with the souring agent.

For example, equal parts of lemon and orange juice and a few dashes of grenadine gives you the Ward Eight (*see* p.204), the only drink to be named after a political constituency.

The tallest member is the Collins, which is basically a Sour with ice and soda water. Then there are Fizzes, which are short Collinses made to be drunk quickly.

But always remember that this is a drink that acts as a wake-up call to the taste buds and so must never, ever be sugary.

Life ain't sweet, it's sour.

THE SOUR

For centuries it has been realized that just a squeeze of lemon juice can transform a spirit. As with any classic mixed drink, sours are at heart essentially simple creations: lip-smackingly refreshing jolts of flavour, perfect either on a summer's afternoon, or as a wake-up call when things are getting a little gnarly late at night. Essentially, they are about harnessing pure flavours, and in their most stripped-down state are barely a cocktail at all, more like a grown-up lemonade. Learn to make a balanced Sour and you can make any drink.

When typing, I've always misspelled Sour as "Spur", which conjures up thoughts of the Anthony Mann/ James Stewart western, *The Naked Spur* – that tough, bitter (sour, even), meditation on humanity and morality. Actually, that seems pretty apposite. If the Manhattan is a *noir* cocktail, then the Sour is a tight, hard-edged B-movie. Just imagine you're Sam Fuller and you'll be okay...

That 2:1:½ ratio is a guideline. This is a drink matched not just to the whisky but to the ability of the consumer (*i.e.* you) to tolerate sourness. I know there is such a thing as Sour mix, but it should be left on the shelf. I mean, how hard is it to squeeze a lemon? Fresh juice is essential. Simple syrup is fine for the sweetening agent. You can add an egg white to create a frothy head and smoothness – but if you are using egg, then shake the Sour like the devil.

RECIPE

orange peel

1 sugar cube

1 tsp water

2–3 dashes of Angostura
or orange bitters

90ml (3fl oz) whisky

In an Old-Fashioned glass, muddle
the orange peel with the sugar, a
little water, and the bitters. Add
whisky and ice cubes. Stir.

THE OLD-FASHIONED

Here is another bona-fide classic. How could you dispute
the pedigree of a drink with such a *respectable* moniker?
Everything speaks of stability, establishment, security,
of things unchanging. It's a drink the secrets of which
a grandfather passes down. A coming-of-age libation.

For many years I've wondered whether the Old-
Fashioned was always old-fashioned. Its name suggests
it's an homage to some ancient style of drink, which
implies that there was an original Old-Fashioned – shiny,
bright, and new... and therefore not old-fashioned.

However, that name is also suggestive of a drink that
may have been popular but is now passé. In this light,
the Old-Fashioned was always old-fashioned, although
doesn't it also invoke warm, fuzzy feelings of simple
times: of log cabins and the frontier spirit, of rocking
chairs on the porch and home-baked pies cooling on
the windowsill? Not old-fashioned, but timeless.

I've got the backing of Al Jolson on that analysis.
In 1935, he starred in a musical called *Go Into Your Dance*
in which he sings: "A Good Old-Fashioned Cocktail
(With a Good Old-Fashioned Gal)". Take it away, Al:
"If you're feeling kind of lonely
And you feel you need a pal,
Have a good Old-Fashioned cocktail
With a good old-fashioned gal."
This is the 1930s and already Al's reminiscing. As he
should, for the Old-Fashioned was once "the cocktail",
"the Bittered Sling", that mix "of any spirit, bitters, and
sugar", and once whiskey was chosen, "the Whiskey
Cocktail" (*see* p.204). This is the drink, therefore, that
started it all, at the beginning of the 19th century –
meaning by the time it picked up its new name 90-odd
years later, it was pretty old-fashioned.

How hard is it to get right? Well, you'd be amazed. The simpler the cocktail, the more important the balance between each element. The problem often starts when too much water is used – it is only there to dissolve the sugar. Any dilution is done by the ice. Use simple sugar? Yes, but then you lose the theatre. Other fruits? No. Muddled fruit is muddled thinking.

The gentle abrasion of sugar against the orange peel releases aromatic oils to scent the drink. Once the sugar is almost all dissolved, slowly add some whisky and some ice. Stir, slowly. Add the rest of the whisky, stir slowly, add ice, stir slowly. Its appropriate that a drink called the Old-Fashioned is a celebration of the passing of time. This is a conversational drink, not to be rushed in its making, or in its consumption – after all, it's STRONG.

RECIPE

Whisky Punch starts by the making of the oleo saccharum *(sugared oil). Spend some time on this part of the process – peeling the lemon with as little white pith as you can manage – and the Punch will be a thing of beauty.*

peel of 1 lemon

55g (2oz) demerara sugar

1.4 litres (2½ pints) boiling water

1 bottle of Powers or Redbreast Irish whiskey

To make the *oleo saccharum,* muddle the lemon peel with the sugar. Set aside for an hour, until all the oils from the peel have been extracted, then muddle once more.

In a heat-resistant bowl add 225ml (8fl oz) of boiling water to the *oleo saccharum.* Stir.

Add the whiskey and then the remaining water to taste.

Serve warm.

(With thanks to David Wondrich)

THE WHISKY PUNCH

There was always a problem for English Punch-drinkers when they headed to Scotland in the 18th century. Not only did they believe that it was a barbarous and uncivilized country, but it was one with an apparently scant knowledge of lemons and, just like omelettes and eggs, they believed that you can't make Punch without lemon juice. Barbarous and uncivilized indeed.

Our friend Captain Burt (*see* p.16) headed into the Highland wastelands nervously clutching his lemons. The carrying of lemons in a bag around your horse's neck was relatively commonplace for travellers in the Highlands in those days. Although the fruit appears in many recipes – and Rum Punches – during this period, its consumption was restricted to the Lowlands. Carrying them north and donating them to your Highland host was considered to be the highest form of gift.

Dr Johnson, never the happiest of men when north of the border (actually, come to think of it, rarely the happiest of men), also remarked on the heinous way in which the Gaels approached the matter of Punch-making. Clearly neither had come across the practice, later outlined by Samuel Morewood, of rowan berries being used as the acidulant.

The irony, of course, was that Scotland was a Punch-drinking nation. But it wasn't just a Whisky Punch-drinking one. In 18th century Glasgow, Rum Punch was the staple beverage of rich and poor alike, which is less surprising than it may initially seem when you consider how important Glasgow was as a sugar- (and slave-) trading port. Rum distilleries existed in the city from the late 17th century onwards – predating any whisky-making.

Anyway, lemons. As the estimable David Wondrich points out in his magisterial tome *Punch*, large amounts

VARIATIONS

Let Jerry Thomas be your guide to making a classic 19th-century Hot Scotch Punch. In his 1862 *Bartenders Guide*, he specifies the use of Islay or Glenlivet malt whisky – showing not only an understanding of flavour, but reflecting the availability of single malt in America at the time.

I'd go for The Glenlivet 12 year old as the mainland malt, and if going down a smokier route, would use either Kilchoman Machir Bay or Talisker 10 year old.

If you wish to make a cold Whisky Punch, make it as opposite, but then refrigerate it. Before serving (in a bowl with a large block of ice) add 90ml (3fl oz) lemon juice.

Thomas also outlines the marvellously named Spread Eagle Punch, which I'd always taken to refer to the state of the drinker after overenthusiastic consumption, but David Wondrich says the moniker refers either to the American national symbol or a stockbroking term.

This is the same as the recipe opposite, except that, as there's twice as much booze, you'll need twice as much *oleo saccharum*.

peel of 2 lemons
115g (4oz) demerara sugar
1 bottle of Rittenhouse rye
1 bottle of Bowmore Legend or
    Caol Ila 12-year-old malt whisky
2.8 litres (5 pints) boiling water

Prepare the *oleo saccharum* as opposite. Add 450ml (16fl oz) of boiling water, followed by the whisky. Dilute with boiling water to taste. Serve warm.

of lemon juice weren't needed for Whisky Punches because they were served warm, which in turn might have something to do with Scotland's occasionally cool climate. Adding the same percentage of lemon juice to a hot Punch would ruin the balance. Yes, lemons were used, but only the peel.

While there are relatively few classic recipes for Whisky Punches, it is a convivial drink that I feel needs to be re-examined and, in the words of an old (English) folk song, all whisky-drinkers should regularly "fathom the bowl".

RECIPE

crushed ice

30ml (1fl oz) simple syrup or gomme (*see* p.185)

90ml (3fl oz) bourbon

6 sprigs of fresh mint

Half-fill a silver Julep cup or Collins glass with crushed ice. Add the simple syrup and bourbon and stir for 20 seconds. Add more ice and stir again until the glass frosts. Top up with more ice so it domes over the top of the glass. Garnish with the mint and drink through a straw.

THE JULEP

This classic started as one of the morning Slings taken in Virginia and probably originally used Cognac, but as the price of imported brandy rose, so whiskey began to be used instead. The use of mint both harks back to Boece's garden (*see* p.14) and shows an understanding of the stimulation given by its scent.

It strikes me as a very civilized drink, the epitome of southern gentility with its serve in a silver cup plus a napkin provided to stop any condensation from dripping onto your hand. But pause for a second. While the Julep is a drink taken by erudite, white-suited men, if you look closely enough at them you can see the grass (mint?) stains on their knees. The wicker chairs have holes in them, the paint on the porch is peeling. All is not as it seems. The Julep is not so much a polite drink, as one imbued with genteel depravity. It's a drink of long, lost afternoons and ripped-up betting tickets, of long vowels and faded dames whose foreheads mimic the cup's pearly beads.

VARIATIONS

You can make a minted simple syrup (*see* p.185), or use the old trick of replacing the sugar element with a liqueur.

RECIPE

30ml (1fl oz) Scotch

30ml (1fl oz) blood orange
(sanguinello) juice

22.5 ml (¾fl oz) Cherry Heering

22.5 ml (¾fl oz) sweet vermouth

Shake over ice and strain into a
chilled cocktail glass.

THE BLOOD & SAND

This glorious Scotch drink first appeared in Harry
Craddock's *The Savoy Cocktail Book* (1930) and is
named after the 1922 Rudolph Valentino movie in which
the matinee idol starred as a doomed matador. There
is something appropriate about this connection to the
corrida in a drink that seems sweetly innocuous when
you look at its components. Cherry brandy? Orange
juice? Sweet vermouth? But behind these distracting,
swirling, flamboyant colours is a hidden blade only seen
when the whisky comes through to spear the tongue.

It can be like the aftermath of a successful charge by
the bull if you don't pay attention to the orange juice.
Sanguinello's tart edge, akin to that of grapefruit, adds
a requisite sting. Making this with a carton of sweetened
orange juice is a waste of time. Try to use the complex
Cherry Heering (or your own cherry whisky (*see* Gean
Whisky, p.187) but never ever use Kirsch. Brand-wise,
Johnnie Walker Black Label (B4), Dewar's 12 year old
(B2), or Great King Street (B2) all work. Lighter choices
don't have the guts required.

RECIPE

90ml (3fl oz) straight rye – I'd go for Sazerac

22.5ml (¾fl oz) simple syrup or gomme (*see* p.185)

Peychaud's bitters

absinthe

lemon twist, to garnish

In a mixing glass, stir together the rye, simple syrup, and liberal dashes of the bitters over ice. Rinse a second glass with absinthe, discarding any left over. Strain the contents of the first glass into it. Garnish with a lemon twist.

Drink with respect.

THE SAZERAC

Like the Julep, this is another whiskey cocktail usurped from the brandy world, a story touching as much on politics – the expulsion of the French from Louisiana – as it does on taste.

It appears to have first emerged as a type of Cognac (or brandy) Old-Fashioned, but was given its name in 1850 when a New Orleans bartender called Sewell Taylor began bringing in Cognac from producer Sazerac de Forge and mixing it in this "old-fashioned" manner. Sewell's bar was then sold to another barkeep, Aaron Bird, who renamed the establishment, "The Sazerac Coffee House", and its signature drink followed suit.

The addition of absinthe appears to have taken place in the 1860s but, by the next decade, with the ravages of phylloxera decimating Cognac production, the base spirit was switched by owner Thomas Handy to straight rye. And so it remains (though it's worth experimenting with Cognac, too).

Whatever the base, this is a drink that speaks of its birthplace: New Orleans. There is something in the fashion in which the murmuring miasmic scent of absinthe and bitters mingle that dips you into the city's louche side. It's a dangerously seductive drink of big flavours, one with just enough sweetness to give you hope for mankind, before the sharp sting of the rye – and it must be rye – comes in like a switchblade, leaving a crimson smear of blood on the bar floor. You take another slug and stagger, glass in hand, into the street. There's music everywhere, faces looming, walls moving. You laugh madly as you weave into decadence's embrace. Like New Orleans, the Sazerac gets into your veins.

CLASSICS

MILLIONAIRE >

60ml (2fl oz) bourbon

15ml (½fl oz) curaçao

7.5ml (¼fl oz) grenadine
or raspberry syrup

egg white

"Vigorously shake the last
three ingredients together,
[over ice] add the bourbon
in three parts, shaking after
each increment. Strain into a
cocktail glass."

(From David A Embury's *The Fine
Art of Mixing Drinks*)

BROOKLYN

60ml (2fl oz) straight rye

30ml (1fl oz) dry vermouth

30ml (1fl oz) sweet vermouth

dash of Amer Picon

dash of Luxardo maraschino

Shake the ingredients over ice
and strain into a cocktail glass.

HUNTER

*This is a drink you'd think
wouldn't work... and yet...*

60ml (2fl oz) Old Ezra 101

30ml (1fl oz) Cherry Heering

dash of Angostura bitters

Stir the ingredients over ice
and serve.

([Re]discovered by Ueno-san of
Bar High Five, Tokyo)

Gaz Regan created a Scotch
variation called the Burnet:
75ml (2½fl oz) Glenmorangie
The Original, 1 tsp Cherry
Heering, Angostura bitters,
and a lemon twist. *See also*
Remember the Maine (p.206).

BARBARY COAST

60ml (2fl oz) bourbon

15ml (½fl oz) orange juice

15ml (½fl oz) sweet vermouth

dash of Yellow Chartreuse

Shake the ingredients over ice
and strain into a cocktail glass.

(From David A Embury's *The Fine
Art of Mixing Drinks*)

WHISKEY COCKTAIL

"*Use a large bar glass*

¾ glass of shaved ice

2 or 3 dashes of gum syrup;
be careful not to use too much

1½ or 2 dashes of bitters
(Boker's genuine only)

1 or 2 dashes of curaçao

1 wine glass of whiskey

"Stir up well with a spoon and
strain into a cocktail glass,
putting a cherry or a medium-
sized olive and squeeze a
piece of lemon peel on top.

"This drink is without doubt
one of the most popular
American drinks in existence."

(Harry Johnson's original 1888 recipe
from his *Bartenders' Manual*

WARD EIGHT

60ml (2fl oz) straight rye

30ml (1fl oz) orange juice

30ml (1fl oz) lemon juice

grenadine, to taste

Shake the ingredients over ice
and strain into a cocktail glass.

WHISKEY DAISY >

"Use a large bar glass

½ tbsp sugar

2 or 3 dashes of lemon juice

dash of lime juice

1 squirt of syphon (soda water); dissolve with the lemon and lime juice

¾ of the glass filled with fine-shaved ice

1 wine glass of good whiskey

fill the glass with shaved ice

½ pony glass (15ml/½fl oz) Yellow Chartreuse

"Stir up well with a spoon; then take a fancy glass, have it dressed with fruits in season, and strain the mixture into it, and serve.

"This drink is very palatable and will taste good to almost anybody."

(Harry Johnson's original 1888 recipe from his *Bartenders' Manual*)

REMEMBER THE MAINE

60ml (2fl oz) bourbon

22.5ml (¾fl oz) sweet vermouth

7.5ml (¼fl oz) cherry brandy

dashes of absinthe, to taste

dashes of Angostura bitters, to taste

Stir over ice (in a clockwise direction) and strain into a cocktail glass.

(From Charles H Baker's *Jigger Beaker, & Glass*)

RUSTY NAIL

The liqueur needs to be matched to the weight – or smokiness – of the Scotch. This is a Scotch drink and not a Drambuie drink.

A variation on this is the Busty Nail made with Laphroaig and Loch Fyne Liqueur. No alternatives work.

75ml (2½fl oz) Scotch

15ml (½fl oz) Drambuie

Stir the ingredients over ice and strain into an Old-Fashioned glass.

FRISCO

60ml (2fl oz) bourbon

15ml (½fl oz) Bénédictine

7.5ml (¼fl oz) lemon juice

Shake the ingredients over ice and strain into a cocktail glass.

(From David A Embury's *The Fine Art of Mixing Drinks*)

SCOTCH HOT-PINT (AKA HET PINT)

"Grate a nutmeg into two quarts of mild ale and bring to the point of boiling.

"Mix a little cold ale with a considerable quantity of sugar and three eggs well beaten.

"Gradually mix the hot ale with the eggs, taking care they do not curdle.

"Put in a half-pint of whisky and bring it once more nearly to boil, and then briskly pour it from one vessel to another till it becomes smooth and bright.

"This beverage carried about in a hot copper kettle is the celebrated Het Pint of Edinburgh and Glasgow."

(From Meg Dods' *The Cook and Housewife's Manual*, 1829)

< ALGONQUIN

60ml (2fl oz) straight
rye whiskey

30ml (1fl oz) dry vermouth

30ml (1fl oz) fresh
pineapple juice

Shake the ingredients over ice
and strain into a cocktail glass.

AFFINITY

30ml (1fl oz) Scotch

30ml (1fl oz) dry vermouth

30ml (1fl oz) sweet vermouth

2 dashes of orange bitters

Shake the ingredients over ice
and strain into a cocktail glass.

BOBBY BURNS

60ml (2fl oz) Scotch

30ml (1fl oz) sweet vermouth

2 dashes of Bénédictine

lemon twist, to garnish

Stir the ingredients over ice
and strain into a cocktail glass.
Garnish with a lemon twist.

For a variation, try using
absinthe or Drambuie instead
of the Bénédictine.

HOT TODDY/HOT WHISKEY v

*The finest Hot Whiskey
I've ever had was in The
Temperance Bar of Malone's
Galtee Inn in Cahir, County
Tipperary – the smallest
whiskey bar in Ireland, if not
the world. It was made to
a "secret recipe" involving
caramelized orange peel,
honey, cinnamon, and Powers.*

150ml (5fl oz) hot water

citrus peel

1 tsp honey

60ml (2fl oz) Scotch or
Irish whiskey

nutmeg (optional)

In a tall glass, add the water
to the peel and honey. Stir to
dissolve. Add the whiskey, stir.
Dust with nutmeg, if liked.

Some people add cinnamon
sticks and cloves. It's up to you.

POLICE GAZETTE

90ml (3fl oz) bourbon

2 dashes of dry vermouth

3 dashes of simple syrup
or gomme (see p.185)

2 dashes of Angostura bitters

2 dashes of curaçao

2 dashes of Luxardo
maraschino

Shake the ingredients over ice
and strain into a cocktail glass.

(Published in *The New Police Gazette
Bartender's Guide*, 1901 and reprinted
in William Grimes' *Straight Up or On
The Rocks*, 1993)

BOULEVARDIER

*The observant among
you will realize that this is
a whiskey Negroni, although
it actually predates that
classic in print.*

45ml (1½fl oz) straight rye

30ml (1fl oz) Campari

30ml (1fl oz) Carpano
Antica Formula

cherry, to garnish

Stir the ingredients over ice in
a mixing glass and strain into
a cocktail glass. Garnish with
a cherry.

(Slightly adapted from Ted Haigh's
Vintage and Forgotten Cocktails)

NEW SPINS

Here are some modern twists on the whisky cocktail from some of the world's most innovative bartenders. The range of – sometimes surprising – ingredients (salmon-infused sherry, anyone?) and the often advanced techniques show how whisky, and bartenders' attitudes towards the spirit, has changed dramatically. It has come off the back shelf and is now regarded as a fascinating and complex package of flavours that are able to be spun into new shapes. It is whisky's complexity compared to vodka's neutrality that is exciting these bartenders the most.

Okay, so some of the techniques described here are not necessarily to be tried at home – instead, seek out the great bars of the world, belly up to the bar, and revel in this rediscovery of whisky.

248 WAYS TO DRINK JW >

60ml (2fl oz) Johnnie Walker Blue Label

1 tsp simple syrup or gomme (*see* p.185) (choice of mandarin, raisin, clove, popcorn, cinnamon, honey, orgeat, sugar, or hazelnut

2 dashes of bitters (choice of Angostura, Peychaud's, orange, cherry, or chocolate) or absinthe

2 cubes of flavoured ice (choice of sweet tea, smoky tea, sherry wood tea, or American oak)

The drinker rolls the dice, spins a roulette wheel, and picks a poker chip out of a hat. The results then dictate which of the simple syrups/bitters/ice cubes will be used. As the name suggests, there are 248 possible combinations.

(With thanks to Tim Philips from Hemmesphere Bar, Sydney, who created this for the final of the 2012 Diageo World Class Bartender of the Year competition)

MATADOR

40ml (1⅓fl oz) Bowmore Darkest

2 dashes of absinthe

2 dashes of orange blossom

1 tsp Luxardo maraschino

1 tsp simple syrup or gomme (*see* p.185)

20ml (⅗fl oz) Cocchi Vermouth di Torino

FOR THE GARNISH

orange twist

cherry

Short shake all the ingredients over ice and strain into a small, pre-chilled cocktail glass. Garnish with an orange twist and a cherry.

(With thanks to Ryan Chetiyawardana of London, who is recognized as one of the country's most innovative bartenders. He is also a whisky fanatic)

CERES JOKER >

Designed to emulate the slight gunpowder/struck-match note found in some sherry and extra-aged spirits, adding a new dimension and a sense of fun to the drink. (Note that the balloon isn't necessary to make and enjoy this drink at home.)

25ml (⁴/₅fl oz) Dalmore 15 year old

25ml (⁴/₅fl oz) sloe gin

15ml (½fl oz) simple syrup or gomme (*see* p.185)

25ml (⁴/₅fl oz) lemon juice

25ml (⁴/₅fl oz) egg white

FOR THE GARNISH

3 dashes of ginger bitters

helium-filled balloon sprayed with lemon essence

Dry-shake all the ingredients without ice, shake with cubed ice and then double-strain into a chilled *coupette* glass. Garnish with the ginger bitters, and the lemon-scented balloon. Tether the balloon to the glass with magician's string. To serve, light the glass end of the string. As the fuse burns, the balloon will rise, and explode, scattering lemon and gunpowder notes around the drink.

(With thanks to Ryan Chetiyawardana)

THE GENTLEMEN'S SECRET

40ml (1¹/₃fl oz) Johnnie Walker Blue Label

15ml (½fl oz) pear liqueur

12.5ml (²/₅fl oz) Pedro Ximénez sherry

6 drops of lavender bitters

sprig of lavender, to garnish

Stir the ingredients over ice and strain into a *coupette* glass. Garnish with a sprig of lavender.

(With thanks to Guiseppe Santamaria of Ohla Hotel, Barcelona, who created this for the final of the 2012 Diageo World Class Bartender of the Year competition)

THE PADOVANI

50ml (1³/₄fl oz) Glenmorangie Signet

15ml (½fl oz) St Germain liqueur

Stir the ingredients over solid rock ice in a tumbler.

(With thanks to Joerg Meyer of Le Lion, Hamburg)

TATAMI COCKTAIL

"Sunlight pours into a Japanese room in the late autumn"

20ml (³/₅fl oz) Yamazaki 12 year old

10ml (½fl oz) crème de cacao

20ml (³/₅fl oz) pineapple juice

5ml (0.16fl oz) apricot brandy

5ml (¹/₆fl oz) fresh lemon juice

1 tsp simple syrup or gomme (*see* p.185)

FOR THE GARNISH

60ml (2oz) Yamazaki 12 year old

blade of lemongrass

Pour the Yamazaki and crème de cacao into a mixing glass and stir over ice. Shake the pineapple juice, apricot brandy, lemon juice, and syrup with ice in a shaker. Strain into a cocktail glass. Float the whisky/cacao mixture on top.

To garnish, pour the Yamazaki into a glass holding the blade of lemongrass. Gently heat the whisky-infused lemongrass over a flame and place in the Tatami glass.

(With thanks to Takayuki Suzuki of the Park Hotel and Shiba Park Hotel, Tokyo. All of Suzuki-san's cocktails take their inspiration from the natural world, and all carry a mention of the season that has influenced their creation)

◄ FIRE OF THE CUILLINS

1 slice of buttered bread

50ml (1¾fl oz) Talisker
10 year old

1 tsp thinly sliced marmalade

10ml (⅓fl oz) simple syrup or
gomme (*see* p.185)

2 dashes of orange bitters

1 egg

Toast the bread. Pour the whisky
over the toast, allow to infuse
for 1 minute, then press the toast
and strain the whisky. Add the
whisky and other ingredients to
a shaker, shake without ice, then
with cubed ice. Double-strain
into a chilled flute.

(With thanks to Ryan Chetiyawardana)

GREEN SUNLIGHT

*"Between summer and fall
in a Japanese vineyard"*

25ml (⁴⁄₅fl oz) Chichibu
3 year old

37.5ml (1¼floz) muscat juice

1 tsp wasabi

Japanese pepper (sansho)
leaf, to garnish

Stir over ice and strain into a
coupette glass. Garnish with
a Japanese pepper leaf.

(With thanks to Takayuki Suzuki)

THE MONARCH

45ml (1½fl oz) The Balvenie
Doublewood

15ml (½fl oz) Lillet Blanc

dash of simple syrup or
gomme (*see* p.185)

absinthe

TO GARNISH

lemon twist

sprig of mint

Stir all the ingredients except
the absinthe over cubed
ice. Rinse a rocks glass with
absinthe, add a block of ice,
and strain the drink over ice.
Garnish with a lemon twist
and sprig of mint.

(With thanks to Ryan Chetiyawardana)

TALISMAN

50ml (1¾fl oz) Talisker
10 year old

20ml (³⁄₅fl oz) fresh
lemon juice

2 tsp nori (seaweed) and
sea salt-infused syrup

2 tsp heather honey

1 tsp Bitter Truth
apricot liqueur

Ground black pepper,
to garnish

Shake the first four ingredients
over ice. Strain into a pre-chilled
cocktail glass rinsed with apricot
liqueur. Garnish with pepper.

(With thanks to Monica Berg,
Acqua Vita, Oslo)

HAZAKURA ᴧ

*"Cherry blossoms have fallen,
revealing fresh green leaves"*

20ml (³⁄₅fl oz) Springbank
10 year old

20ml (³⁄₅fl oz) fresh cream

1 tsp pastis

1 tsp sakura (cherry blossom)
syrup

1 tsp hibiscus syrup

fresh spearmint, to garnish

Shake the ingredients over ice
and strain into a cocktail glass.
Garnish with spearmint.

(With thanks to Takayuki Suzuki)

GREEN BREEZE ʌ

"A forest breeze in the beginning of summer"

As you drink, you inhale the mint, then drink a soda/tonic soft drink, before slowly the whisky and the mint flavours are revealed.

fresh spearmint, plus extra to garnish

5ml (⅙fl oz) white mint liqueur

ice ball

30ml (1fl oz) Hakushu 12 year old

30ml (1fl oz) tonic water

90ml (3fl oz) soda water

Put the mint and mint liqueur in a Collins glass and place an ice ball above. Pour in the Hakushu, then top with tonic and soda. Garnish with mint.

(With thanks to Takayuki Suzuki)

LAPHROAIG SMOOTHIE

30ml (1fl oz) Laphroaig 10 year old

1 tsp Pastis

half a fresh grapefruit

10 leaves of fresh spearmint

2 tsp simple syrup or gomme (*see* p.185)

Blend all the ingredients in a bar blender with ice. Serve in a Collins glass.

(With thanks to Takayuki Suzuki)

PANACEA

50ml (1¾fl oz) Compass Box Asyla

25ml (⅘fl oz) lemon juice

25ml (⅘fl oz) egg white

2 tsp simple syrup or gomme (*see* p.185)

FOR THE SHRUB (you will need 15ml/½oz)

200g (7oz) lavender buds

1½ litres (53oz) cider vinegar

200g (7oz) honey

300g (10½oz) sugar

FOR THE SAGE DUST

20 sage leaves

simple syrup or gomme, to coat

To make shrub, infuse the lavender buds in the cider vinegar *sous vide* for 2 hours at 40°C (104°F). Strain, cook on a medium heat for 30 minutes, then sweeten with the honey and sugar.

To make the sage dust, coat the sage leaves in simple syrup, dehydrate in a low oven or a dehydrator, then grind in a pestle and mortar and sieve with a tea strainer.

Dry-shake all the ingredients in a shaker without ice, then shake hard with ice. Double-strain into a chilled *coupette* glass and garnish with a small sprinkling of sage dust.

(With thanks to Ryan Chetiyawardana)

PAISLEY PATTER >

40ml (1⅓fl oz) Great King Street

dash of grapefruit bitters

2 tsp elderflower cordial

3 sprigs of tarragon

soda

lemon twist, to garnish

Build the whisky, bitters, and cordial over cubed ice in a Sling glass. Stir, add more ice and the tarragon, and top with soda. Garnish with a lemon twist.

(With thanks to Ryan Chetiyawardana)

BAMBOO LEAF MARTINI

"Between the end of winter and the beginning of spring"

Yuzu is a Japanese citrus fruit. If you cannot find it, try grapefruit and lime.

1 tsp white mint liqueur

30ml (1fl oz) Hakushu 12 year old

30ml (1fl oz) still mineral water

2 tsp simple syrup or gomme infused with bamboo leaf (*see* p.185)

FOR THE GARNISH

yuzu twist

bamboo leaf

Pour the mint liqueur into an ice-filled mixing glass. Stir to coat the ice, then discard any excess liqueur. Add the whisky, water, and bamboo syrup. Stir and strain into a cocktail glass that's been lined with a bamboo leaf. Garnish with a yuzu twist.

(With thanks to Takayuki Suzuki)

GREAT GUNNERSBURY BREAKFAST

35ml (1¼fl oz) Great King Street

1 tsp Pierre Ferrand Dry Curaçao

2 dashes of Angostura bitters

fresh raspberries, to garnish

FOR THE PORRIDGE-OAT SODA

50g (1¾oz) porridge oats

vanilla pod

1 tsp salt

1 litre (1¾ pint) water

To make the porridge-oat soda, heat the oats with the vanilla pod and salt in the water at 65°C (149°F) for 40 minutes. Strain the mixture, sweeten to taste, and carbonate in a soda syphon.

Build the whisky, curaçao, and bitters over cubed ice in a Highball glass. Stir, top with more ice, and fill with the porridge-oat soda. Garnish with the raspberries.

(With thanks to Ryan Chetiyawardana)

THE ESTIVAL MANHATTAN

50ml (1¾fl oz) Sazerac Rye Whiskey

20ml (⅗fl oz) Noilly Prat Ambré

1–2 dashes of Fee Brother's Peach Bitters

Stir the ingredients and serve in a cocktail glass.

(from Mario Kappes, Le Lion, Hamburg)

SKYE & SEA >

60ml (2fl oz) Talisker

15ml (½fl oz) fino sherry that has been briefly cold-infused with salmon, lavender, and mixed spice

2 dashes of Peychaud's bitters

dash of rhubarb bitters

Talisker-marinated salmon, to garnish

Shake the ingredients over ice and strain into a cocktail glass. Serve the salmon on the side.

(With thanks to Kae Yin of Marsalis, Taipei City, who created this for the final of the 2012 Diageo World Class Bartender of the Year competition)

MAJOR SOURCE BIBLIOGRAPHY

Baker Jnr, Charles H. *Jigger, Beaker, & Glass*. New York: Derrydale Press, 1992.

Bannerman, John. *The Beatons: A Medical Kindred in the Classical Gaelic Tradition*. Edinburgh: John Donald, 1998.

Bell, Darek. *Alt Whiskeys: Alternative Whiskey Recipes and Distilling Techniques for the Adventurous Distiller*. Nashville: Corsair Artisan Distillery, 2012.

Boece, Hector. *The History and Chronicles of Scotland*. Publisher unknown, 1526 (reprinted Edinburgh: W&C Tait, 1881).

Brown, Jared & Miller, Anistatia. *Spiritous Journey: A History of Drink, Books 1 & 2*. Cheltenham: Mixellany Books, 2010.

Buchan, James. *Capital of the Mind: How Edinburgh Changed the World*. London: John Murray, 2003.

Burt, Capt Edmund. *Letters from a Gentleman in the North of Scotland*. Edinburgh: Ogle Duncan & Co, 1822.

Buxton, Ian. *The Enduring Legacy of Dewar's: A Company History*. Glasgow: Angel's Share, 2009.

Carson, Gerald. *The Social History of Bourbon*. Kentucky: University Press of Kentucky, 2010.

Chambers, Robert. *Traditions of Edinburgh*. Edinburgh: W&R Chambers, 1869.

Chisnall, Edward. *The Spirit of Glasgow: The Story of Teacher's Whisky*. Location unknown: Good Books, 1990.

Cooper, Ambrose. *The Complete Distiller (1757)*. London: Vallient, 1757.

Craddock, H. *The Savoy Cocktail Book*. London: Constable & Co, 1930.

Daiches, David. *A Wee Dram: Drinking Scenes from Scottish Literature*. London: André Deutsch, 1990.

Daiches, David. *Scotch Whisky: Its Past and Present*. London: André Deutsch, 1969.

de Kergommeaux, Davin. *Canadian Whisky: The Portable Expert*. Toronto: McClelland & Stewart, 2012.

Dods, Margaret. *The Cook and Housewife's Manual: A Practical System of Modern Domestic Cookery and Family Management*. Edinburgh: Oliver & Boyd, 1829.

Dornat, C.C. *The Wine and Spirit Merchant's Own Book A Manual for the Manufacturer and a Guide for the Dealer in Wines, Spirits, Liqueurs, Etc.* London: Raginel Domenge, 1855.

Duplais, P & McKennie, M. *A Treatise on the Manufacture and Distillation of Alcoholic Liquors Comprising Accurate and Complete Details in Regard to Alcohol from Wine, Molasses, Beets, Grain, Rice, Potatoes, Sorghum, Asphodel, Fruits, Etc.* Philadelphia: Henry Carey Baird, 1871.

Embury, David A. *The Fine Art of Mixing Drinks*. New York: Doubleday, 1958.

The Filson Historical Society. *The Filson News Magazine Vol.6, No.3*, "19th-Century Distilling Papers at The Filson". Louisville: Kentucky, 2006.

Fouquet, Louis. *Bariana: Receuil Practique des Toutes Boissons Americaines et Anglaises*. Paris: publisher unknown, 1896 (reprinted Cheltenham: Mixellany Books, 2008).

Grant, Elizabeth. *Memoirs of a Highland Lady*. London: John Murray, 1911 (reprinted Hong Kong: Forgotten Books, 2012).

Grimes, William. *Straight Up or On The Rocks: The Story of the American Cocktail*. New York: North Point Press, 2001.

Haigh, Ted. *Vintage Spirit & Forgotten Cocktails*. London: Quarry Books, 2009.

Janson, Charles William. *The Stranger in America*. London: James Cundee, 1807.

Johnson, Harry. *The New and Improved Bartenders' Manual*. New York: I Goldman, 1900, (reprinted Cheltenham: Mixellany Books, 2009).

Johnson, Samuel, & Boswell, James. *Journey to the Hebrides: A Journey to the Western Islands of Scotland & the Journal of a Tour to the Hebrides*. London: Canongate, 1996.

Lacour, Pierre. *The Manufacture of Liquors, Wines and Cordials Without the Aid of Distillation.* New York: Dick & Fitzgerald, 1853.

MacDonald, Aeneas. *Whisky.* New York: Duffield & Green, 1934.

MacLean, Charles. *Scotch Whisky: A Liquid History.* London, Cassell, 2003.

Martin, Martin. *A Description of the Western Islands of Scotland.* London: Andrew Bell, 1703.

McNeill, F Marian. *The Scots Cellar: Its Traditions and Lore.* Edinburgh: Reprographia, 1973.

Moran, Bruce T. *Distilling Knowledge: Alchemy, Chemistry and the Scientific Revolution.* Massachusetts: Harvard University Press, 2005.

Morewood, Samuel. *A Philosophical and Statistical History of the Inventions and Customs of Ancient and Modern Nations in the Manufacture and Use of Inebriating Liquors.* Dublin: W. Curry Jun. and W. Carson, 1838.

Morrice, Philip. *The Schweppes Guide to Scotch.* Sherborne: Alphabooks, 1983.

Moryson, Fynes. *An Itinerary Containing His Ten Yeeres Travell through the Twelve Dominions of Germany, Bohmerland, Sweitzerland, Netherland, Denmarke, Poland, Italy, Turky, France, England, Scotland & Ireland.* Glasgow: James MacLehose & Sons, 1907.

Moss, Michael S & Hume John R. *The Making of Scotch Whisky A History of the Scotch Whisky Distilling Industry.* Edinburgh: James & James, 1981.

Mulryan, Peter. *The Whiskies of Ireland.* Dublin: O'Brien Press Ltd, 2002.

O'Neil, Darcy. *Fix The Pumps.* Ontario: Art of Drink, 2010.

Odell, D. *Mixing It Up, A Look at the Evolution of the Siphon-Bottle.* Location unknown: Digger Odell Publication, 2004.

Pacult, F Paul. *A Double Scotch How Chivas Regal and The Glenlivet Became Global Icons.* New Jersey: John Wiley & Sons, 2005.

Pennant, Thomas. *A Tour in Scotland and Voyage to the Hebrides, 1772.* London: Benjamin White, 1776.

Regan, Gary & Mardee. *The Book of Bourbon and Other Fine American Whiskeys.* Vermont: Chapters Publishing Ltd, 1995.

Regan, Gary. *The Joy of Mixology: The Consummate Guide to the Bartender's Craft.* New York: Clarkson Potter, 2003.

Schmidt, William. *The Flowing Bowl: What and When to Drink.* New York: Charles L Webster, 1891 (reprinted New York: Mud Puddle Inc, 2010).

Sinclair, Andrew. *Prohibition: the Era of Excess.* London: Little, Brown, 1962.

Smout, T.C. *A Century of the Scottish People 1830-1950.* London: Fontana, 1990.

Sulz, Charles Herman. *A Treatise on Beverages, or The Complete Practical Bottler.* New York: Dick Fitzgerald, 1888.

Tarling, William J. *Café Royal Cocktail Book.* London: United Kingdom Bartenders Guild, 1937 (reprinted Cheltenham: Mixellany Books, 2008).

Thomas, Jerry. *Bartenders Guide, or How to Mix Drinks.* New York: Dick & Fitzgerald, 1862 (reprinted Paris: Vintagebook, 2001).

Thorndike, Lynne. *History of Magic and Experimental Science, Vol IV* (chapter on Michael Scot) New York: Columbia University Press, 1934 (reprinted Montana: Kessinger Publishing, 2009).

Tovey, Charles. *British & Foreign Spirits: Their History, Manufacture, Properties, Etc.* London: Whitaker & Co, 1864.

Wilson, C. Ane. *Water of Life: A History of Wine-distilling and Spirits 500 BC to AD 2000.* Devon: Prospect Books, 2006.

Wilson, John. *Noctes Ambrosianae, Vol III.* New York: WJ Widdelton, 1863.

Wondrich, David. *Punch: The Delights (and Dangers) of the Flowing Bowl.* New York: Perigee, 2010.

INDEX

Page references in *italics* indicate illustrations

THANKS

PICTURE CREDITS

Mitchell Beazley would like to acknowledge and thank all those whisky companies and their associates who have kindly provided images for this book.

Cocktail photographs are by Cristian Barnett for Octopus Publishing.

Additional photographs:

Alamy David Hancock 65; David Lyons 58; Hemis 47, 52; Heritage Image Partnership 25; Ilian food & drink 84; Squib 60

The Art Archive Eileen Tweedy 13

Bridgeman Art Library Science Museum, London 18

Cephas Mick Rock 48

Courtesy **Chivas Brothers** 29, 68

Corbis Ocean 62

Courtesy **Cutty Sark International** 8

Courtesy **The Edinburgh Whisky Stramash** www.thewhiskystramash.com 7

Courtesy **Edrington**, photo Peter Sandground 57

Courtesy **Fever-Tree** www.fever-tree.com 63, 64

Getty Images Aaron Ontiveroz 2; AFP 6, 11, 41; Bloomberg via Getty Images 4, 49; Gary Latham/Britain on View 12; Margaret Bourke-White/Time & Life 36; Monty Rakusen 42; Siân Irvine 182; The Washington Post 59, 184

Library of Congress 35; **Mary Evans Picture Library** 17, 31

Press Association Images Danny Lawson/PA Archive 51

Courtesy **Savoy Group Archives** 37

Shutterstock Jaime Pharr 43; Aleix Ventayol Farrés 54

Thinkstock iStockphoto 45

TopFoto City of London/HIP 22

The University of Aberdeen 14

Courtesy **Vita Coco** www.vitacoco.co.uk 67

Courtesy **The Whiskey Ice Co** www.whiskey-ice.com 61

To my fellow usquebaugh-imbibing heretic, Ryan Cheti, for sparing his time and technical knowledge to help me explore some of the more recherché areas of whisky history and for creating all the drinks for the cocktail shoot. This book would not have been possible without him.

Thanks to everyone who contributed samples. Special thanks to Stephen Marshall, Jason Craig, John Glaser, and Chris Maybin, for more whisky than I could have possibly imagined, and to Charles Rolls and Tim Warrilow at Fever Tree, for the marvellous magical mixers, without which this book wouldn't exist.

To Jim Beveridge, Maureen Robinson, Gordon Motion, Kirsteen Campbell, Brian Kinsman, and Shinji Fukuyo, for showing me the world and mind of the blender.

To Jonathan Driver and Stuart Kirby, for a memorably game-changing night in Rio. David Croll, for many long evenings scouring Japan for the perfect drink. John Hansell, Amy Westlake, Lew Bryson, and all on *Whisky Advocate*, for New York immersion.

To friends, for their ears as I babbled semi-coherently about various theories: Jared and Anistatia, for their endless enthusiasm and for always being a fantastic sounding board; Iain Russell and Nick Morgan, for sober(ish) historical perspective; Davin de Kergommeaux, for his knowledge of Canadian whisky; Dave Wondrich, Gaz Regan, Bum, and Annene, and other fathomers of the bowl. Marcin Miller, Neil Ridley, Joel Harrison, Gavin Smith, Olly Wehring, Johnny Ray, Tim Forbes, Rob Allanson: you know what you are.

To all the battle-scared survivors of Tales of the Cocktail, especially Tris Stephenson, Andy Gemmell, Stu McCluskey, Tom Walker, Jason Scott, Anette Moldvaer, Georgie Bell, Nick Strangeway, Keshav Prakash, and Sophie Decobecq. Music upstairs... always.

To the World Masterclass team, Tim, Dale, Fasie, Chief, and Two-Mile, for unforgettable road trips.

To Mark Ridgwell, for his passion for education – which has allowed me to form various mad theories in the guise of teaching – and to those victims who had to listen to them; and to Sukhinder Singh, Thierry Benitah, and the whisky chicks in South Africa, for allowing me to do the same.

To all involved in the Malt Advocates Course, the greatest whisky "university" in the world, which teaches me something new every time I attend.

To the Malt Maniacs, for keeping the flame burning and doing it with such good humour and passion; to Serge Valentin and Michel van Meersbergen, for maintaining a weekly flow of out-there jazz.

To the countless barkeeps who have poured me a drink over the years, but especially to Nick Strangeway, who has always been there, and Takayuki Suzuki, the Zen master of cocktails and a dear and true friend who always knows when I should be in bed. To Angus and Kae in Taipei City, who opened up a new world of whisky culture for me, and Naren Young, for Manhattans on tap.

A massive thank you to Denise Bates at Octopus, who has been the calmest and most helpful of editors; to Hils, Leanne, and Juliette – the A-Team is back together! – and to Cristian Barnett, for his amazing cocktail images.

To my agent, Tom Williams, for assistance beyond the call of duty and the calm voice of reason at times of despair.

Lastly to my wife, Jo, for not only coping (again) with the madness of book-writing, but for her palate, patience, and immense help in co-ordinating the tsunami of whisky that arrived on our doorstep; and to our daughter, Rosie, who knew when to give me a hug and when to roll her eyes.